THE BÁb & BaHÁ'u'llÁh

Jenabe E. Caldwell

Best Publisher
Wailuku, Hawaii
http://www.bestpublisher.org

The Story of the Báb and Bahá'u'lláh
Jenabe E. Caldwell

Best Publisher
Wailuku, Hi
http://www.bestpublisher.org

© Jenabe E. Caldwell
All rights reserved

Cover design by Jenabe E. Caldwell

2nd Edition

ISBN 0-9762780-1-4

First Edition Published in Japanese 1995
ISBN 4-88866-239-8

CONTENTS

Foreword..4

Chapter 1	Shakyh Ahmad & Siyyid Kazim	6
Chapter 2	Declaration of the Báb	21
Chapter 3	Bahá'u'lláh	37
Chapter 4	Báb Continued	42
Chapter 5	Bab in Isfahan	56
Chapter 6	Bab's Journey	62
Chapter 7	Mullá Husayn	73
Chapter 8	The Báb in Chihriq	76
Chapter 9	Fort Tabarsi	81
Chapter 10	Darkness before Dawn	101
Chapter 11	Remnant of God	120
Chapter 12	Táhirih	133
Chapter 13	King of Glory	146

FOREWORD

Who was this Bahá'u'lláh, this man that could touch the hearts and minds of primitive people up to the highest leaders of the world? More than 30,000 Bahá'ís from every corner of the planet came to New York for a conference in the fall of 1992. At the same time conferences were being held in Panama, New Delhi, Australia, Samoa, Russia, Germany and Israel.

What kind of person was Bahá'u'lláh that He was able to bring so many different kinds of people together in love, and unity? What power did He have to start something that in just 100 years has brought into being the fastest growing community in the world today? Magnificent buildings have been constructed in every continent in His name. An International Centre has been established with some of the most beautiful gardens in the world. Bahá'u'lláh's followers number in the millions. There are National Assemblies in 172 countries. Schools, hospitals, refugee camps, environmental offices and other humanitarian institutions are being started and operated by Bahá'u'lláh's followers. At the beginning of the United Nations in New York, the Bahá'ís have been part of and hold advisory positions on most of the non governmental organizations.

Who was Bahá'u'lláh? Where did

Bahá'u'lláh come from? Where did Bahá'u'lláh live? How did Bahá'u'lláh live? What happened to Bahá'u'lláh? We will attempt to answer these questions in the book.

Chapter 1
Shaykh Ahmad & Siyyid Kazim

Shaykh Ahmad

Our story begins in Bahrain a small island in the Persian Gulf. Bahrain lies off the coast of Saudi Arabia. The city was Ahsá and the date was May 24, 1743. Shaykh Ahmad was born. We have little information about the early life of this great and holy man. After much soul searching and seeing what Islam had become Shaykh Ahmad said that he was called by God to go into the world and prepare mankind for the coming of two great messengers of God. Alas, for we have no record of how this call came. Shaykh Ahmad wrote ninety-six books and it is hoped that future writers will be able to tell us the exact information of how this call to service came to this great man.

Shaykh Ahmad was very sad and heartsick at the divisions, sects and fighting and wars among the so-called followers of this Divine Light, Muhammad. Shaykh Ahmad had spent the first 40 years of his life studying Islam. He fully realized that only a new and pure teaching from God could change the hearts of man. From his deep study of the teachings of Muhammad he had decided that the time promised for the coming of these new teachers was now. He also learned that not one great teacher was to come but in this day of God Himself, two great lights would come into the world. The call of

God that came to Shaykh Ahmad, was that he must go into the world and prepare the hearts of man as much as possible to accept these twin Spiritual Teachers that were soon to come.

He left Bahrain and his island home and family in 1783 at the age of forty. His first stop was in Karbilá, a city about 55 miles southwest of Baghdad where he started classes and he drew many students. These also very quickly increased. The students came from far distant places. Soon he was admitted into the ranks of the mujtahids (highest priest) and was known far and wide as an Imam. He was considered one of the most learned and smartest of the priests in Islam. His fame spread rapidly in Iran and Iraq. Because of the fanatical minds of the people, Shaykh Ahmad had to be very careful in his purpose of informing his following of the soon to come two great teachers of mankind. In Islam in the Qur'án and the stories of Muhammad it was clearly stated that two would come.

Much like John the Baptist crying in the wilderness during the coming of Christ, so Shaykh Ahmad was for the Báb and Bahá'u'lláh. Because all of his teachings were based on the Holy Qur'án and scriptures he became very famous in that part of the world. His school and ideas are still being taught up to the present day and his followers are called Shaykhs

Shaykh Ahmad was well loved and respected by everyone that met him, from lowly peasants to the highest government officials. He traveled on foot from Bahrain to Najaf then to Karbilá. There were no cars, trains or airplanes in those days, so people either went on foot or by horse. Shaykh Ahmad always knew that he was directed and guided by the hand and inspiration of God. He then went on and visited Mashad.

Mashad had the fame of being one of the most holy cities and also the worst of cities. The pilgrims (people that go to a special place to pray) that came to this holy place would, with the help of the priests, make a deal for temporary wives. These women would be married to the pilgrim until they left the city. Then they would be married again to another pilgrim and so on.

From Mashad he went on to Shiraz. In Shiraz, to the amazement of his followers, he praised the city of Shiraz, as the best of cities and when asked, what made Shiraz so special, he told his followers to just be patient and soon its glory would be understood by all. The Báb was born in Shiraz on October 20th, in 1819, and declared Himself in 1844 in Shiraz, to speak for God and to close the door on the past and open the door for this age. The glory spoken by Shaykh Ahmad for this city was then understood.

Then Shaykh Ahmad went on to Yazd and Nayin always fearlessly calling the people to prepare themselves for the coming very soon of the two great messengers that were promised to appear at the end of time. The King of Persia wrote to Shaykh Ahmad with some questions and was so happy with Shaykh Ahmad's answers that he invited him to the capital as his guest.

While in Yazd and Nayin a man named Mahmud heard about one of the students of Shaykh Ahmad and went to see him and was instantly converted to the cause of Shaykh Ahmad. Mahmud explained that one morning at dawn he found this student fallen on his face and praying. The student explained to Mahmud that the new messenger of God had been born. That day was the 12 of November 1817. The time of the birth of Bahá'u'lláh was that day at dawn.

Shaykh Ahmad then went on to Khurasan and from there to the capital of Tihrán. The Shah of Persia when he was told that Shaykh Ahmad was coming sent a delegation of high government officials to meet him and escort him with all honors into the capital city. As the light of the new day touched the eastern sky on November 12, 1817, Shaykh Ahmad was in the city of Tihrán. He was aware of the birth of Bahá'u'lláh and longed to spend the rest of his life near Him in Tihrán. However the eldest and favorite son of the King told his father that he wanted this famous holy man Shaykh Ahmad to come to Kirmanshah as his guest. The King granted this request and sent Shaykh Ahmad his orders to go to Kirmanshah.

He then went on and lived for sometime in

Kirmanshah a guest of the eldest son of the Shah. He was there until the prince died. S͟hayk͟h Ahmad then returned to Karbilá and there he selected his most sincere and devoted followers and prepared them to accept the forth coming messenger from God. It was in Kirmanshah that S͟hayk͟h Ahmad once again taught all of his followers that when he died all were to turn without any reservation to Siyyid Kazim for their guidance and direction. In his writing at this time he referred over and over again to Ali and Husayn. This reference was to Ali Muhammad (the Báb) and Husayn Ali (Bahá'u'lláh) there can be no doubt about this as Ali, the son-in-law of Muhammad was in the past as was the Imam Husayn. The references of S͟hayk͟h Ahmad referred to the future. This was just another evidence of this great and holy mans divine inspiration. S͟hayk͟h Ahmad then went to Mecca and Medina. He passed away in Medina at the age of 82 in 1834.

Siyyid Kázim

The title Siyyid means a person whose parents, grandparents, great grandparents and so on come from the Prophet Muhammad. Siyyid Kázim was born in Rasht in the province of Gilan in 1793. At the age of 11 Siyyid Kázim had memorized the whole of the Qur'án. At the age of 14 he had further memorized many stories about Muhammad and prayers. At the age of 18 he wrote his first book and at the age of 22 he left home and family and became a student of Shaykh Ahmad. One night as Siyyid Kazim was drifting between sleep and wakefulness, he suddenly became aware of someone in the room with him. He recognized one of the saints ancestors. The saint told him to go to Yazd and to put himself under the spiritual guidance of Shaykh Ahmad.

Shaykh Ahmad told Siyyid Kazim that he had been waiting for him to come. After only a few weeks Shaykh Ahmad turned over all of his classes to Siyyid Kázim before he left for Khurasan. This favor from this exalted and famous teacher to Siyyid Kazim caused some envy and jealousy among some students, but such was the knowledge, wisdom and saintliness of Siyyid Kazim that they were all won over to him.

When Shaykh Ahmad went to visit the King of Persia in Tihrán, he took Siyyid Kazim with him. Although Siyyid Kazim wanted to go with Shaykh Ahmad to Mecca and Medina, he was not allowed to go. His teacher explained that the time for the new messenger was now so close that there was no time to lose in preparing the people for His coming.

With the passing of the saintly and holy Shaykh Ahmad, Siyyid Kazim found himself the target of constant hate and a victim of slander, envy and jealousy. The clergy came together with the plan to destroy not only Siyyid Kazim, but the teachings of Shaykh Ahmad as well. They knew that they were powerless in the face of the distinguished and powerful Imam Shaykh Ahmad. Now, however with him no longer on the scene they were sure that they could destroy Siyyid Kazim and the teachings of such a powerful teacher as Shaykh Ahmad. Siyyid Kázim was appointed the new leader after Shaykh Ahmad.

Shaykh Ahmad had the support not only of the King but also his title of mujtahid. Siyyid Kázim had neither and as a result the powerful corrupt clergy thought that they could destroy not only Siyyid Kázim but also the teachings of Shaykh Ahmad. At this time the most powerful religious figure of the time in that part of the world was living and teaching in Isfahan. Siyyid Kázim in order to continue the preparation of the people for the coming of the twin light's of God, was inspired to try to get the support of this powerful clergyman in Isfahan.

Siyyid Kazim chose Mullá Husayn as his messenger and sent him off to Isfahan to secure the support of this famous leader. Mullá Husayn was a young man, 28 years of age, who had recently been enrolled as a student of Siyyid Kazim. The title Mulla indicates a priest of the Muhammadan Faith.

When Mullá Husayn arrived in Isfahan he went directly to the famous leader's home. The Siyyid Baqir, was busily engaged in teaching the many students that were present. The place was magnificent and the congregation were all important men of note and all were richly dressed. Mullá Husayn, on the other hand, was travel stained and his clothes were of the simplest type, also showing much wear from his long and hard trip from Karbilá all the way to Isfahan.

Mullá Husayn worked his way through that high class crowd to a place facing the seat of the renowned and famous teacher, Siyyid Baqir. Then with humility, yet with confidence and power Mullá Husayn said, "Listen, O Siyyid, to my words for your response to my message will ensure the safety of the Faith of the Prophet of God, Muhammad, and your refusal will cause it grievous injury." These bold and courageous words spoken with directness and force, caught the full attention of this famous and renowned Siyyid Baqir. He now ignored completely his audience and gave his total attention to his disheveled and strange visitor. Some students of Siyyid Baqir tried to interrupt Mullá Husayn, some even got angry and tried to denounce him. With extreme politeness, and in firm and dignified language, Mullá Husayn hinted at their discourtesy. He Mentioned a verse of the Qur'án of Muhammad that they were to show honor and courtesy to the stranger. The Siyyid was very pleased with the politeness and dignity of this stranger and he apologized for the bad behavior of his students. The Siyyid also in order to show a proper attitude towards strangers as an object lesson to his students went even further in his response and kindness to

Mullá Husayn.

This great teacher had been keeping silent as regards both Shaykh Ahmad and Siyyid Kazim because he had many questions about what they were teaching. Mullá Husayn was able to answer all of Siyyid Baqir's questions to the Siyyid's complete satisfaction and he wrote a letter to Siyyid Kazim in full support of Siyyid Kazim's teachings. He also testified to the purity of heart of the youthful messenger Mullá Husayn. It was noted by the assembled grandees that this esteemed and honorable teacher often had tears in his eyes when he listened to Mullá Husayn speaking with such love, sincerity and respect yet with a humility and force that moved him to his very soul.

When Mullá Husayn left, Siyyid Baqir had a servant follow him to where he was staying. The servant reported back that Mullá Husayn had retired to a dingy little room with only a thin worn mat on the floor and not even a blanket to cover him. Siyyid Baqir then sent the servant to Mullá Husayn with a very large sum of money and apologizing for not having given him the accommodations that he should have. Mullá Husayn sent the money back with a message that this fair minded and just Siyyid Baqir had given him a gift more precious than all the gold and silver in the world, which was a just, fair and honest interview and a letter to help further the Cause of God.

Mullá Husayn dispatched the letter to

Siyyid Kazim by messenger and received a loving letter in reply. The letter to Mullá Husayn left no doubt that Siyyid Kazim knew of his coming death and was bidding Mullá Husayn goodby.

Siyyid Kazim knew who the Báb was and the following account can leave no doubt about this.

One day at the hour of dawn one of the close and trusted students of Siyyid Kazim was suddenly awakened and ordered to go to the Siyyid's house. Upon his arrival they found the Siyyid fully dressed and waiting for him. The student was told that a very important and distinguished person had arrived in Karbilá and they were going to visit him. They then went to a house in Karbilá and at the door was a young Man waiting for them. This young Man had on a green turban a sign of His holy linage. He very fondly embraced Siyyid Kazim with great affection. Siyyid Kazim who was used to meeting the highest and most prominent dignitaries and had even been in the court of the King, seemed to be overcome with humility and joy upon meeting this Youth. The attitude of Siyyid Kazim could only be described as a deep and loving reverence toward this young Man. He then led us into the house to an upper floor that had many flowers and the fragrance of a loveliest perfume. He told us to sit down. He then filled to the brim a silver cup that was on the table and gave it to Siyyid Kazim, with these words from the Qur'án, "A drink of a pure beverage shall their Lord give them." Although it is forbidden by the faithful of Islam to drink from a silver cup, Siyyid Kazim without any hesitation and in a state of holy rapture and delight, drank. Our youthful host then offered me a drink from that same cup but no words were said. All that was spoken was the above quoted verse. He then led us to the door and bid us farewell. The student was mute with wonder at the charm and bearing of that Youth, that radiant face, that melodious voice and the delicious beverage which He gave them. A few days later the student saw that same young Man come into Siyyid Kazim's class and take a seat near the door. As soon as Siyyid Kazim saw this Youth enter the room he stopped his lecture. When one of the students pleaded with Siyyid Kazim to continue, He said, "What more can I say, the truth is more manifest than that ray of sunlight that has fallen upon that lap." When the student looked, he saw that indeed a ray of sunlight had fallen upon the lap of the young Man. The student found out that the youth was a merchant from the city of Shiraz.

Later that same student was privileged to be a secretary to the Báb. The student's name was Hasan and he had been a student of Shaykh Ahmad and Siyyid Kazim, he became a devoted follower of the Báb and when a very old man he was privileged to meet and recognize Bahá'u'lláh in Karbilá long before Bahá'u'lláh's declaration. The Báb had sent this Hasan to Karbilá with explicit instructions that he was to stay there until he would meet the promised Husayn. He was then to give this promised Husayn the Báb's assurances of His love. The words' Bahá'u'lláh said to Hasan when they met in Karbilá was, "Praise be to God that you have remained in Karbilá, and have beheld with your own eyes the face of the promised Husayn." Over all these years Hasan had never told anyone of the instructions given to him by the Báb.

The enemies of Siyyid Kazim were not silenced by the letter from this leading divine of Isfahan that had been secured by Mullá Husayn. This seemed to increase their fury and jealousy. Through slander and plotting they gathered up a large following. The clergy and the ruffians they had enlisted, ousted the government official from Karbilá and stole all of this official's property. Of course the central government immediately dispatched a military force to Karbilá to put down this rebellion.

Because Siyyid Kazim was an important and a much loved person, the official in charge of the military force sent a communication to Siyyid Kazim. The official asked Siyyid Kazim to try to pacify the excited people and to counsel them to moderation and to submit to the authority of the central government. If they were to follow his instructions he further guaranteed the people's safety and protection.

When Siyyid Kazim received this official

communication, he called together the chief instigators of this rebellion and gave them the message from the leader of the military force. While in the presence of the Siyyid these rebels feigned submission and agreed to accompany the Siyyid to the military camp in the morning. They were aware that if they submitted to Siyyid Kazim that his fame and authority would be greatly increased. So the clergy plotted and said that they had dreams and that if their followers waged a holy war against the army, that the army would be defeated. When Siyyid Kazim realized their plots he dutifully notified the commander of the army. At this point the army sent a final order to surrender by morning and if they did not the army would attack and the only safe place in the city would be the home of Siyyid Kazim. Siyyid Kazim upon receipt of this message had it announced throughout the city.

The rebels were completely overthrown the following morning and the streets of Karbilá ran with blood. The holy shrines of the Imam Husayn and Imam Abas which are normally secure safe places were not spared. The only place that was safe was at the home of Siyyid Kazim. So big was the crowd that came, several adjacent houses were taken over to protect the vast number of people at his house. That strange and mysterious event took place on January 10, 1843.

Every year, from November 23 to December 23, Siyyid Kazim would go to Kazimayn from Karbilá. As was his custom he departed Karbilá on November 23, 1843. He had a large number of his followers that accompanied him. On the 4th day of his travel, Siyyid Kazim stopped along the road to offer the mid-day prayer. Siyyid Kazim had just finished his prayer when suddenly an Arab shepherd appeared and came right up to Siyyid Kazim and hugged him. "Three days ago," he said, "I was shepherding my flock in this adjoining pasture, when sleep suddenly fell upon me. In my dream I saw Muhammad, the Apostle of God, He told me, 'Listen to my words shepherd and treasure them within your heart. For these words of Mine are the trust of God which I commit to your keeping. If you are faithful to them, you will receive a great reward. If you are not, you will have just as great troubles. Now listen carefully; this is My trust to you: Stay here in this place. On the third day, a member of my house, a Siyyid Kazim by name along with many friends will stop at noon and he will offer his noon-time prayer at this spot. As soon as you see him, you are to go to him and give him My most loving greetings. Tell him, from Me:

"Rejoice, for the hour of your departure is at hand. When you return to Karbilá on December 31, you will wing your flight to Me. Soon after you depart this life, He who is the Truth shall be revealed. Then the world will be lit up by the light of His face.'"

Siyyid Kazim's followers were very

saddened by this news. This great holy and inspired teacher told them that they should not be sad for didn't the messenger say that the new light of God would then break over the world. The Historian that recorded this event got the information from at least ten of the followers who were present on that occasion. So it happened. Upon Siyyid Kazims return to Karbilá he fell ill. As the lowly shepherd said he passed on to the great beyond at the age of 60, on December 31, 1843. He was buried in Karbilá near the shrine of the Imam Husayn.

CHAPTER 2
Declaration of The Báb

Mullá Husayn returned to Karbilá on January 22, 1844. He found all the followers of Siyyid Kazim saddened and with no leader. Some of these followers of Siyyid Kazim told Mullá Husayn that they thought he was the one promised by Shaykh Ahmad and Siyyid Kazim, because of the high praise which Siyyid Kazim always had when referring to Mullá Husayn. Mullá Husayn denied this most strongly stating that his knowledge was not even a drop or a speck of dust compared to the sun of the knowledge of the Promised One.

Mullá Husayn then invited the followers of Siyyid Kazim to his home and asked them to tell him what the last instructions of his beloved teacher Siyyid Kazim were. All of them agreed that his last wishes were that they leave everything and scatter far and wide in their search for the Promised One of God. The door to His Holy and Divine Presence was now wide open. Those with a pure heart and pure motives would be led to Him through prayer and sincerity.

Mullá Husayn looked around the room at all these great and distinguished persons and asked the question. If what you say is true then why are you all sitting here.

One said, "I have a shop and I must look

after my shop."

Another said, "I am a doctor and I have many sick people that need me, I surely can't be expected to go."

And yet another, "I have my pigs and chickens. Who will feed my pigs and chickens if I go?"

A student said, "I have important exams and if I went what about my important exams. Surely you can't expect me to go."

And so it was throughout the room. Although Siyyid Kazim had most strongly said leave everything, even your homes and families and go seek out the Light of God that was now to light up the world, they all had their excuses.

As I write this it is many years later. Who was that shop keeper? No one knows and no one cares. The same thing goes for the doctor, the student and the keeper of the pigs and chickens. They have all gone the way of Mullá Husayn. That is to their graves every one. However, Mullá Husayn got up and went and that is the only difference. The name of Mullá Husayn is already known around the world and parents from the most remote jungles to the most great cities are naming their babies after this great and holy man. The name of Mullá Husayn is destined to be remembered on this earth for the next 500,000 years.

Mullá Husayn then visited all the followers in Karbilá of Siyyid Kazim that had not attended the meeting and in a loving, humble and sincere way urged them one and all to follow the instructions to the letter of their recently departed leader.

Mullá Husayn went to his mother and sister and lovingly explained the situation. He informed them that he would leave them in the hand of God to protect and look after them. Both of Mullá Husayn's loved ones encouraged him to do what God had planned. Both of these women became devoted followers of the Báb and attached to that lioness of the Cause of God "Táhirih" the only women destined to become one of the Báb's letters of the living.

Mullá Husayn with only his brother and nephew left Karbilá and took the road north. They stopped at a rooming house and Mullá Husayn started 40 days of prayer, meditation and fasting. This he did to prepare himself for his holy search in finding the Holy One that was now ready to be revealed to the world. The peace and calm that descended on that place was interrupted by the arrival of 12 other followers of Siyyid Kazim from Karbilá that had decided to do as Mullá Husayn had done. Every time anyone tried to talk to Mullá Husayn they found him so deep in his prayers that they felt they could not disturb him. So after talking it over they all decided to do the same thing that Mullá Husayn was doing and they started their own 40 day fasting and praying.

At the end of his fast Mullá Husayn with

his brother and nephew left. As if drawn by an unknown and mysterious power, with a force that he could not resist, Mullá Husayn with his two fellow travelers arrived at the outskirts of the city of Shiraz in Iran. Mullá Husayn sent his brother and nephew ahead into the city to make the arrangements for food and a place to stay in this city. Mullá Husayn told his companions that he would join them in the center of town in time for the evening prayer, God willing.

This wonderful spiritual man was strolling outside the city and as always praying most fervently that God would guide him to the Promised One. Suddenly he saw coming towards him a young man wearing a green turban that signified that he was a Siyyid and a descendent of the Prophet Muhammad. He walked right up to Mullá Husayn and embraced him. Mullá Husayn was surprised by this unexpected event. Who was this stranger he had never seen before and why was he treating him as if he were a dear friend? These questions ran through his mind. Then he thought, well maybe this stranger would lead him closer to the Holy One he was looking for. Maybe God had sent him to aid him in his search.

This stranger overwhelmed Mullá Husayn with love and kindness and gave him a most loving invitation to come to his home and refresh himself after his long journey. Mullá Husayn thanked the stranger, but explained that his brother and nephew were waiting for him to join them for evening prayers. The stranger said, "Commit them to the care of God, He will surely protect and watch over them." He then told Mullá Husayn to follow him and Mullá Husayn was powerless to resist this radiant and most magnetic personality. He was compelled by that same mysterious power that had drawn him to the outskirts of this city to humbly follow this mysterious stranger to his home. As Mullá Husayn followed him even the way the stranger walked impressed him with his dignity and bearing.

When they arrived at a simple house, the stranger knocked on the door which was soon opened by an Ethiopian servant. The stranger then said a verse from the Qur'án, "Enter therein in peace secure." and he led Mullá Husayn into the house. This verse said with such power and majesty touched the very soul of Mullá Husayn. Mullá Husayn felt that this was a good sign from heaven because he was about to enter his first house in Shiraz with the words of God echoing in his heart and mind.

This story was related to a number of people by Mullá Husayn himself so let's let Mullá Husayn tell the rest of the story:

"Might not my visit to this house, I thought to myself, enable me to draw nearer to the Object of my quest? Might it not hasten the termination of a period of intense longing, of strenuous search, of increasing anxiety, which such a quest involves? As I entered the house and followed my Host to His chamber, a feeling of unutterable joy invaded my being. Immediately we were seated, He ordered an ewer of water to be brought, and bade me wash away from my hands and feet the stains of travel. I pleaded permission to retire from His presence and perform my ablutions in an adjoining room. He refused to grant my request, and proceeded to pour the water over my hands. He then gave me to drink of a refreshing beverage, after which He asked for the samovar and Himself prepared the tea which He offered me."

"Overwhelmed with His acts of extreme kindness, I arose to depart. 'The time for evening prayer is approaching,' I ventured to observe. 'I have promised my friends to join them at that hour in the Masjid-i-Ilkhani.' With extreme courtesy and calm He replied: 'You must surely have made the hour of your return conditional upon the will and pleasure of God. It seems that His will has decreed otherwise. You need have no fear of having broken your pledge.' His dignity and self-assurance silenced me. I renewed my ablutions and prepared for prayer. He, too, stood beside me and prayed. Whilst praying, I unburdened my soul, which was much oppressed, both by the mystery of this interview and strain and stress of my search. I breathed this prayer, 'I have striven with all my soul, O my God, and until now have failed to find Thy promised Messenger. I testify that Thy word faileth not, and that Thy promise is sure.'"

"That night was the evening of May 22, 1844. It was about an hour after sunset when my youthful Host began to converse with me. 'Whom, after Siyyid Kazim,' He asked me, 'do you regard as his successor and your leader?'

'At the hour of his death,' I replied, 'our departed teacher insistently exhorted us to forsake our homes, to scatter far and wide, in quest of the promised Beloved. I have, accordingly, journeyed to Persia, have arisen to accomplish his will, and am still engaged in my quest.'

'Has your teacher,' He further enquired, 'given you any detailed indications as to the distinguishing features of the promised One?'

'Yes,' I replied, 'He is of pure lineage, is of illustrious descent, and of the seed of Fatimih. As to His age, He is more than twenty and less than thirty. He is endowed with innate knowledge. He is of medium height, abstains from smoking, and is free from bodily deficiency.'"

"He paused for a while and then with vibrant voice declared: 'Behold, all these above mentioned signs are manifest in Me!' He then considered each or the above-mentioned signs separately, and conclusively demonstrated that each and all were applicable to His person."

"I was greatly surprised, and politely observed: 'He whose advent we await is a Man of unsurpassed holiness, and the Cause He is to reveal, a Cause of tremendous power. Many and diverse are the requirements which He who claims to its visible embodiment must needs fulfil. How often has Siyyid Kazim referred to the vastness of the knowledge of the promised One! How often did he say: 'My own knowledge is but a drop compared with that with which He has been endowed. All my attainments are but a speck of dust in the face of the immensity of His knowledge.' Nay, immeasurable is the difference!"

"No sooner had those words dropped from my lips than I found myself seized with fear and remorse, such as I could neither conceal nor explain. I bitterly reproved myself, and resolved at that very moment to alter my attitude and to soften my tone. I vowed to God that should my Host again refer to the subject, I would with the utmost humility, answer and say, 'If you be willing to substantiate your claim, you will most assuredly deliver me from the anxiety and suspense which so heavily oppress my soul. I shall truly be indebted to you for such deliverance.' When I first started upon my quest, I determined to regard the two following standards as those whereby I could ascertain the truth of whosoever might claim to be the promised Qaim. The first was a treatise which I had myself composed, bearing upon the abstruse and hidden teachings propounded by Shaykh Ahmad and Siyyid Kazim. Whoever seemed to be capable of unraveling the mysterious allusions made in that treatise, to him I would next submit my second request, and ask Him to reveal, without the least hesitation or reflection, a commentary on the Surih of Joseph, in a style and language entirely different from the prevailing standards of the time. I had previously requested Siyyid Kazim in private, to write a commentary on that same Surih, which he refused to, saying: 'This is verily beyond me. He, that great One, who comes after me will, unasked, reveal it for you. That commentary will constitute one of the weightiest testimonies of His truth, and one of the clearest evidences of His position.'" (This conversation with Siyyid Kazim about the story of Joseph, Mullá Husayn said that he never mentioned it to anyone and was hidden alone in his mind.)

"I was revolving these things in my mind, when my distinguished Host again remarked: 'Observe attentively. Might not the Person intended by Siyyid Kazim be none other than I?''

"I thereupon felt impelled to present to Him a copy of the treatise which I had with me. 'Will you,' I asked Him, 'read this book of mine and look at its pages with indulgent eyes? I pray you to overlook my weaknesses and failings.' He graciously complied with my wish. He opened the book, glanced at certain passages, closed it and began to address me. Within a few minutes He had, with characteristic vigor and charm, unraveled all its mysteries and resolved all its problems, Having to my entire satisfaction accomplished, within so short a time, the task I had expected Him to perform, He further expounded to me certain truths which could be found neither in the reported sayings of the Imams of the Faith nor in the writings of Shaykh Ahmad and Siyyid Kazim. These truths, which I had never heard before, seemed to be endowed with refreshing vividness and power."

"'Had you not been My guest,' He afterwards observed, 'your position would indeed have been a grievous one. The all-encompassing grace of God has saved you. It is for God to test His servants, and not for His servants to judge Him in accordance with their deficient standards. Were I to fail to resolve your perplexities, could the Reality that shines within Me be regarded as powerless, or My knowledge be accused as faulty?'"

The Báb picked up His pen and told Mullá Husayn that it was time to reveal the book about the true meaning of the story of Joseph. As Siyyid Kazim had said the promised One would reveal it to Mullá Husayn unasked. So it was done. Mullá Husayn sat enraptured not only by the uninterrupted flow of the writing but also by the gentle chanting of the Báb as He revealed the verses. The heavens of revelation had been cleft a sunder. The voice of God was once more being heard in this physical world. The first person in the world to become a believer in these new teachings from God was this same Mullá Husayn. The Báb told Mullá Husayn, that if he was to leave in his present state everyone would think that he had lost his mind. The exact time of the Báb's declaration as the mouth piece of God, was two hours and eleven minutes after sunset. According to their calendar the day begins at sunset, so the day was May 23, 1844.

The Ethiopian servant appeared and served dinner at the third hour after sunset. The food was the most delicious food Mullá Husayn had ever eaten he said that this heavenly meal had fed his soul as well as his body. This first meeting lasted the entire night. Mullá Husayn was startled by suddenly hearing the call to morning prayers. Mullá Husayn was instructed by the Báb to go to the center of Shiraz and set up classes and to be engaged in teaching and prayers. He was commanded by the Báb not to tell any soul who the Báb was. The Báb explained that a total of eighteen souls through their prayers and sincerity must seek Him out and find Him on their own as Mullá Husayn had done. He told Mullá Husayn that from time to time He would join his classes and that Mullá Husayn was not to betray His identity by any act or word even to Mullá Husayn's brother and nephew. The Báb also told Mullá Husayn that He was going to Mecca and Medina and that one of these eighteen souls must go with him on this trip. Mullá Husayn then went to meet his brother and nephew and as instructed began to teach.

This new divine message and Holy

Messenger hit Mullá Husayn like a thunderbolt. His whole being was electrified. He was filled with awe, joy, wonder and excitement. His body had even become transformed. He felt a new strength flowing through him. He felt that the whole universe was a mere handful of dust that he held in the palm of his hand. Mullá Husayn had said that before he had felt timid and his walk and hand trembled when he walked or wrote. After the revelation of the Báb these problems had completely disappeared.

Bahá'u'lláh had said that all knowledge consisted of twenty seven letters, and from Adam to Muhammad only two letters had been given to man by God. The Báb revealed the other twenty five letters of knowledge. All the messengers of God are equal, but the amount of revelation that the Báb gave to mankind was more extensive than any of the others were permitted to give.

Mullá Husayn then following the instructions of the Báb, started his classes. The spirit of Mullá Husayn was so strong and he gave such beautiful explanations that more and more people from all parts came to hear him. On a number of days the Báb would invite Mullá Husayn to his house. Mullá Husayn would, on those nights from dusk to dawn sit at the feet of the Báb, wakeful and in a state of heavenly bliss. On one such visit the Báb informed Mullá Husayn that the next day thirteen of Siyyid Kazim's followers would arrive. Mullá Husayn was to provide them with a most loving welcome and assist them in whatever way he could. Mullá Husayn was again told not to in any way give away the secret of having found the Divine, Holy and most loved Mouth-piece of God. The very next day as the Báb had said the thirteen people arrived.

In the same manner as Mullá Husayn had done in finding the Báb, slowly after a period of 40 days, seventeen holy souls had found the Báb by their own unaided efforts. Once again drawing on that holy and divine spirit that moved within Him the Báb informed Mullá Husayn that the last one to be enrolled would come on the following evening. In the evening of the next day a young man only 22 years old appeared and when Mullá Husayn tried to talk to him, he told Mullá Husayn that he already recognized the Báb by the way He walked. He further told Mullá Husayn that no one else on earth besides the Báb, who he saw there, could claim to be this promised One. When Mullá Husayn told this to the Báb, the Báb explained to Mullá Husayn that in the world of the spirit this young man had been for a long time in communication with Him and they knew each other very well. This young man, the last one, was named Quddús. These first 18 people that found the Báb and enrolled as His followers were known at Letters of the Living. Only one of them, who was a woman, never met the Báb in person. She was known as Táhirih and when Táhirih's sister's husband decided to go and seek this new promised messenger of God, Táhirih gave her bother-in-law a letter to give to this mouth-piece of God when he found him. She informed him that he would find this promised one. In this letter she explained that in the world of the spirit she recognized Him and was ready to sacrifice her life in His service. Táhirih was more firmly convinced of the truth of the new message by a dream she had. In this dream a young man with a green turban was standing in heaven and was chanting a verse. Táhirih woke up and wrote one of the verses she had heard in her notebook. Later when some of the first writings of the Báb were given to her, to her great delight, one of the Báb's verses was exactly the one she had written down in her notebook.

These eighteen Letters of the Living hold a station more higher and of greater importance than the twelve disciples of Jesus. Each of them was given a task and sent off in different directions to teach others about the Báb and to prepare the way for the coming of Bahá'u'lláh. Fortunately we live in a day of better communication and as a result we have more information about this Holy Manifestation of God than any of the messengers of the past.

The Báb sent Mullá Husayn towards the north from Shiraz. He told Mullá Husayn that in Tihrán he would find a light that would be even greater than the one he had found in Shiraz. The Báb then chose Quddús to go with him to Mecca and Medina.

Mullá Husayn was not given a name or address of this person in Tihrán. He was told that God would guide him to this hidden Jewel in that capital city. The Báb gave Mullá Husayn a written tablet to deliver to this unknown person. The Báb's parting words to Mullá Husayn were very powerful. The Báb said, "The essence of power is now dwelling in you, and the company of His chosen angels revolves around you. His almighty arms will surround you, and His unfailing Spirit will ever continue to guide your steps. He that loves you, loves God; and whoever opposes you has opposed God. Whoso befriends you, him will God befriend; and whoso rejects you, him will God reject."

Once Mullá Husayn had arrived in Tihrán he went to the school of the Shaykhi's in that city. The leader of that school and the leader of the Shaykhi community in Tihrán treated Mullá Husayn with contempt and disrespect. One of the students, who had overheard the conversation between Mullá Husayn and the teacher of that school, was instantly attracted to Mullá Husayn and could not believe that his teacher was so closed minded. When this student later came to Mullá Husayn it was through him that Mullá Husayn was led to Bahá'u'lláh. This student knew Bahá'u'lláh and often visited His home. So now Mullá Husayn asked the student to deliver the tablet from the Báb to Bahá'u'lláh.

This student, Mulla Muhammad has

recorded that event in his own words: "As I approached the house of Bahá'u'lláh , I recognized His brother Mirza Musa, who was standing at the gate, to whom I communicated the object of my visit. He went into the house and soon reappeared bearing a message of welcome. I was ushered into His presence, and presented the scroll to Mirza Musa, who laid it before Bahá'u'lláh. He glanced at its contents and began to read aloud to us certain of its passages. I sat enraptured as I listened to the sound of His voice and the sweetness of its melody. He had read a page of the scroll when, turning to His brother, He said, 'Musa what have you to say? Verily I say, whoso believes in the Qur'án and recognizes its Divine origin, and yet hesitates, though it be for a moment, to admit that these soul-stirring words are endowed with the same regenerating power, has most assuredly erred in his judgment and has strayed far from the path of Justice.'

CHAPTER 3
Bahá'u'lláh

Bahá'u'lláh's instant acceptance of the teachings of the Báb started a new chapter in the revelation of God's Holy Manifestation. Bahá'u'lláh immediately and most vigorously started to inform the people of Iran about this new and wondrous teaching. Bahá'u'lláh's social position, was at that time, the very highest. He come from a noble family dating far back into history, his family descent was from Zoroaster and from Abraham's wife Katurah. He had, through His love and kindness to the poor and underprivileged, become known throughout the land as the father of the poor. Bahá'u'lláh traveled very far and in all directions to share this wonderful teaching with His country men.

The historian Cheyne said, "Bahá'u'lláh's speech was like a 'rushing torrent' and His clearness of exposition brought the most learned divines to their feet." An uncle of Bahá'u'lláh tried to stop his nephew and stated that whoever met Bahá'u'lláh fell immediately under His spell, and was enthralled by what He said. This uncle said that either Bahá'u'lláh was a sorcerer, or He mixed some mysterious substance in the tea that made the people who drank it to fall a victim to Him. The person that was told this then asked Bahá'u'lláh's uncle, how come he didn't fall a victim too as he had been in Bahá'u'lláh's presence and also drank Bahá'u'lláh's tea.

On one of Bahá'u'lláh's teaching trips as He was riding through the countryside he saw a man, his hair all messed up as was his clothes. When Bahá'u'lláh came to the place He found this man busy with a fire cooking and eating. When Bahá'u'lláh asked him what he was doing, the man replied that he was cooking and eating God. Bahá'u'lláh got off of His horse and joined the man alongside his fire. With love and gentleness Bahá'u'lláh explained the Unknowable greatness of God and the creator of all that is or ever will be. Bahá'u'lláh's love, kindness and explanation so won over this man that he left his pots, food and possessions and on foot he followed after Bahá'u'lláh's horse singing and making up poetry about the love he had found and the true knowledge of God Bahá'u'lláh had given him.

Bahá'u'lláh was born in Tihrán at dawn on November 12, 1817. He was born into a royal family. One of the King's ministers was Bahá'u'lláh's father named Abas and his mother was Khadíjih Khánum. Bahá'u'lláh's father was known as Mirza Buzurg and he was the governor over a large area. Mirza Buzurg was known for his honesty, fairness and justice.

One day Bahá'u'lláh's father had a very extraordinary dream. He dreamt that his son, Bahá'u'lláh was swimming in a vast ocean, His body shone upon that sea like the sun. His body shone so brightly that it lit up the sea. Then His father noticed his son's head. It was out of the water and His jet black hair in great profusion floated upon the water. Attached to each and every strand of hair was a fish, yet his son moved in what ever direction He wanted to go upon this sea and neither the fish nor the waves could slow down His movement.

Bahá'u'lláh's father was greatly impressed by this dream and he sent for a famous man that knew how to interpret dreams. This fortune teller or soothsayer explained. The sea was the sea of life and represented the whole world and everything in it. He then explained that Bahá'u'lláh would rule single and alone, supreme over the whole world. The fish represented the entire human race and one and all they would one day cling to Bahá'u'lláh for safety and protection. No matter how vast the number of people there were and the turmoil they would be in, they would never be able to slow or hinder in any way the cause or purpose of Bahá'u'lláh.

One of the famous divines of Iran that knew Bahá'u'lláh also had a dream that he recorded. He explained that in his dream he had come upon a room filled with trunks which he was told belonged to Bahá'u'lláh. When this divine opened the trunks he found them filled with books and the writing in the books were made of the most brilliant jewels and shone with such dazzling beauty and brightness that he woke up.

As a baby Bahá'u'lláh was a special child, never crying and never restless. Bahá'u'lláh never attended any school and this was proven by the people that knew Him. Bahá'u'lláh's knowledge, deep understanding and wisdom came from within Him. As a small child Bahá'u'lláh went to a wedding and part of the show was furnished by a famous puppeteer named Sultan Salim. Bahá'u'lláh stood and watched fascinated by the tiny puppets that danced and sang and went through a real life drama. The joys, trials, triumphs and defeats of life were skillfully portrayed by Salim. The audience went through these events sometimes with laughter, sometimes with tears and all enraptured by the story told on the stage. Bahá'u'lláh although only a child followed all the happenings with the greatest interest. After the show Bahá'u'lláh went back to thank this man on his most wonderful performance. Sultan Salim was very busy putting things away and preparing to leave. Bahá'u'lláh asked him where were all those wonderful life like beings He had seen in the show. Sultan Salim pointed to a box and said that they were all in the box. Bahá'u'lláh, although at the earliest stage of His childhood, said that at that moment He understood the emptiness of life spent in the pursuit of material gain and of this world. Like the puppets of Sultan Salim one day we would all end up in the box and of what value was all our games, plans, schemes, successes and failures.

As a child, a youth and a young man Bahá'u'lláh was always courteous and patient. He had a rare understanding and at the age of 14 He was already famous throughout the land as having this understanding. Bahá'u'lláh was a master of speech and argument and no one was better at explaining things than Him. Bahá'u'lláh loved nature and the country and in His childhood and youth He spent most of His time in the fields.

Once Bahá'u'lláh accepted the Báb, He never turned aside from His commitment and dedication to this Cause of God. All of His days were used to the fullest to promote these new teachings and to prepare mankind for the soon to be revealed coming divine revelation.

CHAPTER 4
Báb Continued

The Báb received Mullá Husayn's letter informing Him of Bahá'u'lláh's instant declaration. He also told the Báb about His teaching efforts in other places. Mullá Husayn especially explained about the efforts and traveling teaching trips that Bahá'u'lláh had done on His own. The Báb, along with Quddús and his Ethiopian servant, then left Shiraz for the pilgrimage to Mecca and Medina. When the Báb reached the center of pilgrimage, a place called the Ka'bah he grasped the ring on the door and three times in a loud and majestic voice declared:

"I am the Qá'im whose advent you have been awaiting." This public declaration caused a sudden hush to fall upon those near enough to hear Him. Like a stone dropping into the water, that sudden and majestic declaration, once set in motion it cascaded outward in ever-widening circles until it has now encircled the earth.

The Báb also sent a written declaration to the Sharif of Mecca, one of the leading officials of that place of pilgrimage. This leader did not reply. Later in a conversation this Sharif explained that he was too busy at the time and only read the book sent him by the Báb after the season of pilgrimage was over. It was too late for him to find out any more information about the Báb. If we are ever too busy for God, we are busier than God wants us to be.

Some of the pilgrims that came from Shiraz carried the news of the Báb's declaration with them when they returned. As stated this ever-widening circle generated by His declaration not only gained new followers of the Báb, but also brought about fierce arguments. Some were ready to investigate and others were intent on not only the destruction of the Báb, but also of His followers and teachings.

The Báb had relatives in Bushihr and He also had done business there as a merchant, so He stayed there for a short time. He sent Quddús on to Shiraz with letters to His uncle, wife and mother. The Báb told them that He had safely returned from His pilgrimage and would be home to Shiraz soon. Quddús also had with him some of the Báb's teachings. Quddús met the Báb's uncle and shared with him these teachings and what He had been taught by the Báb on their nine month trip together to Mecca and Medina. The Báb's uncle gave his heart, life and soul to his nephew. The wife of the Báb was the first in the family to recognize Him, and this uncle, Siyyid Ali was the second.

Quddús also met in Shiraz a follower of the Báb Ismullah Asdaq whom had been sent to Shiraz by Mullá Husayn. Quddús shared some of the Báb's teachings with this Ismullah. One of the things the Báb had said was to proclaim to everyone His name and the name of Bahá'u'lláh. This Ismullah fearlessly did that from the mosque (church). The opposition had already been organized by some of those that had returned from pilgrimage and so Quddús and Ismullah were arrested. The governor of the province ordered that they each be given a thousand lashes with the whip. He further ordered that they put holes in their noses and pass a cord through the holes. Like a cow with a ring in its nose, they were to be paraded through the streets of Shiraz then put out of the city with instructions that if they ever returned they would be put to death. Asdaq Ismullah was a man very advanced in years and everyone that witnessed this inhuman torture was sure that he would die before 50 lashes of the whip had been given. Witnesses verified that Ismullah was seen to be covering his mouth with his hand as the whip was being applied with strength and vigor. Although Ismullah's back and shoulders were a mass of torn flesh, he not only withstood the whipping but seemed to glow with a spirit or radiant joy. Later several of the witnesses came to him and asked him why he was covering his mouth and how was he able to bear such horrible torture. He explained that the first seven strokes of the whip were extremely painful. The other nine hundred and ninety three did not seem to touch him. It was as if they were applying the whip to a distant post, not to his body. He said that he was covering his face so that he would not laugh. Ismullah's faith was strengthened because he fully realized that God was indeed protecting him. After the beatings the holes were cut in their noses and they were paraded through the streets of Shiraz and kicked out of the city.

This unjust and horrible punishment had the effect of proclaiming the name and the mission of the Báb to the entire population of Shiraz and also to the whole of Iran. It was reported in a newspaper in London and as far away as America. These articles have been found and verified.

The governor was not satisfied with this, but sent an armed guard to Bushihr to arrest the Báb and bring Him back to Shiraz in chains. The soldiers were about forty kilometers from Bushihr when they discovered a Siyyid with an Ethiopian servant coming to meet them. The Báb asked the leader of the soldiers what they were looking for. The leader gave an evasive answer. The Báb told the soldiers that they had been sent to arrest Him. The Báb said that He didn't want them to go to so much trouble and so He had come out to meet them. This way He had saved them a long and hard trip. The soldiers were amazed and tried to get the Báb to run away and save himself from the wrath of an inhuman governor. The Báb refused saying that God was directing Him and His path was through Shiraz. The Báb's gentleness, courtesy and loving kindness completely won over the soldiers. He entered Shiraz, not in chains and humiliated as the governor had wanted, but at the head of the soldiers as a hero. This parade further proclaimed to all the message of the Báb.

A number of people in Shiraz were becoming followers of the Báb and the talk of everyone was either for or against Him. The Báb was taken directly to the house of the governor. Without any questions or investigation this governor insulted the Báb. The Báb answered this governor with His usual dignity and respect. Of course this further infuriated this mean governor and he had an attendant strike the Báb in the face. The Báb's uncle Siyyid Ali came and paid the bail for the Báb's release. This the governor agreed to and let the Báb go on the terms that the Báb address the public from the mosque and repudiate His claim.

Again this announcement that the Báb was going to speak at the mosque was a further proclamation for His Divine Cause. On the required day the mosque was overfilled. Every available space was crowded with an eager audience. When the Báb began His address, as was His custom, He began with the glorifications and praises of God. One of the altar boys interrupted with, "stop this idle chatter and say what you have to say." The church leader told the boy to hold his tongue. The Báb then in a clear and majestic voice proclaimed that he was not a go between of the promised Qa'im. He upheld with all His heart and soul the truth of the prophet Muhammad. He loved and respected the twelve Holy Imams of the Faith. The Báb and His uncle returned to their home, but the governor put the Báb under house arrest. The Báb was indeed the Promised One Himself and not a go between.

When the followers of the Báb learned of His condition they began to come, a few at a time, to Shiraz to meet Him at His uncle's house. One evening when three believers were with the Báb, the Báb turned to one of the three and in a very sweet and tender voice said, "Abdul Karim are you seeking the Manifestation?" This Abdul Karim threw himself at the feet of the Báb and wept, he was completely out of control. The Báb picked up Abdul Karim and comforted him.

Later, when the three were alone they asked this Abdul Karim what that was all about. Abdul Karim then told the following story: He had wanted to understand the mystery of God and of His saints and prophets and so he had started to study every branch of human learning. He had enrolled with the best and most learned religious leaders he could find. Day and night he studied until one day his teacher declared that Abdul Karim no longer needed to attend his classes. He was to be elevated in rank to the highest religious order in Iran. He was quite proud and even his family were planning to give him a big party.

Then Abdul Karim began to have second thoughts. He said to himself that he had thought these lofty divines were free from all error. Now he was sure that like him because of their pursuit of knowledge they had lost sight of the search. Deep in his heart and in conversation with his soul he knew that he had not gotten any answer to his question as to the mystery of God or His saints and prophets. His first reaction was a soul felt prayer for forgiveness. Then another heart felt prayer for God to guide him. Suddenly he seemed to be in a room with a Siyyid who was speaking with such wisdom and force to a large group of students. Then he was back in his own room. The next day he went to one of his friends and when he explained about the Siyyid, this friend told him who he was talking about was Siyyid Kasim who was teaching in Karbilá.

Abdul Karim and his brother, the next day left for Karbilá and found Siyyid Kasim exactly as he had found him in his vision. Siyyid Kasim was even talking about exactly the same thing. Of course Abdul Karim enrolled in his class. Siyyid Kasim sent Abdul Karim and his brother back to his home with a firm promise that he would find the promised one.

Every night Abdul Karim would pray fervently that God would guide him to the new manifestation of God as was promised by Siyyid Kasim. One night after his prayer he seemed to have fallen into a trance. There appeared a beautiful white bird and it flew about his head and landed on a branch near him. The bird in a sweet and tender voice asked him if he was seeking the manifestation. This experience was so sweet that he thought about it all the time but never shared it with any other soul. The night that he first came to see the Báb, he had heard that same sweet and tender voice say exactly what he had heard in his vision. That was why his reaction to the Báb was so dramatic.

This ever widening circle of proclamation of course reached the capital and the attention of the King. At that time there was living in Tihrán the most distinguished divine in all of Iran. He was a guest of the King. This divine, named Vahíd, had memorized over thirty thousand traditions of Muhammad. At what ever meeting Vahíd was at, he was always the chief speaker. He was renowned not only for his vast knowledge and his memory, but also for his mature judgement and wisdom. Any of the divines that had the courage to challenge him were totally defeated. The King had absolute confidence in Vahíd's judgement, impartiality, competence and spiritual insight. It was natural for the King to send Vahíd to Shiraz to do a full and in depth investigation of the situation. Vahíd was also very anxious to gain this first hand knowledge and was very happy to receive the King's request.

Vahíd was convinced that when he met the Báb, he would have no trouble in putting the Báb in his place. On the trip to Shiraz, Vahíd day dreamed about how he would take this imposter back with him to Tihrán as an evidence of his ability. Upon

Vahíd's arrival, as he had been sent on the King's mission, he was a guest of the hostile and hated governor. He also met an old time friend of his named Azim. Azim had become one of the devoted followers of the Báb and he told Vahíd to be very careful and respectful when he met the Báb.

Vahíd met the Báb at the Báb's uncle's house. For about two hours Vahíd asked questions in great depth about the most difficult passages of the Qur'án. The Báb sat quietly and listened. The Báb then gave short and concise answers to all the questions. Vahíd realized that he had been showing off in expressing his great knowledge and learning. He was overcome with shame at his ego and pride. He left that first meeting ashamed and humbled. The time before the next interview Vahíd spent in thinking about questions that would prove or disprove the Báb's claim to be the promised Qaim.

Vahíd was horrified to discover that when he came into the room with the Báb that he had completely forgotten all his questions. Vahíd's mind was like a photographic mind and all his life he never forgot anything. Then to his wonder and amazement he heard the Báb answering all the questions he had forgotten. Vahíd was so shaken to his very heart and soul that he begged permission to leave and fled. His friend Azim met him and Vahíd explained that it might just be a coincidence. Azim said that he wished that schools had never been invented because such learning kept us back from the fountain of God which was the Báb.

Vahíd then determined that at the next interview in his inmost heart he would request the Báb to explain in writing one of the verses of the Qur'án called the Surih of Kawthar. He would not make this request openly and he shared this determination with no one. Kawthar refers to a lake or river in Paradise which Muhammad saw on His mystic night journey.

As was the case with Mullá Husayn when he asked the Báb for proof. It is God's place to test His creatures, not the creature's place to test their God. When Vahíd came into the room with the Báb this time he became terrified. Vahíd's body shook with terror. Vahíd the divine that had been many times in the presence of the King had never felt even the slightest awe or fear, was now completely overcome. The Báb seeing the condition of Vahíd got up and taking his hand helped him to a seat. Vahíd said he felt like a baby and could not even speak. The Báb then said in a loving and tender voice that if he was to reveal the commentary on the Surih of Kawthar would Vahíd recognize that he was neither a soccer nor a magician and his words came from God. Vahíd wept and the tears flowed as he heard the Báb and the only words Vahíd could speak was a verse from the Qur'án. "O our Lord, with ourselves have we dealt unjustly: if Thou forgive us not and have not pity on us, we shall surely be of those who perish."

The Báb then asked His uncle for pen and paper and began to write without any pause or for-thought the explanation of the Surih of Kawthar. The Báb did not stop until the book was completed. Vahíd sat amazed and bewildered at this outpouring of divine revelation. Tea was served and then the Báb began to read aloud what He had written. Vahíd was so overcome by emotion that several times he was on the point of fainting. He was revived by the Báb sprinkling rose water on his face. The Báb then left and told His uncle that Vahíd was to stay in the uncle's home while they verified the book. The Báb's secretary and Vahíd took three days and three nights to check and verify all the traditions in the text. The whole book was verified and was absolutely correct. Vahíd had attained a state of complete certitude and free of doubts. Vahíd from that moment to the end of his life dedicated every breath, heart-beat and his soul to the Cause of God as found in the person of the Báb.

The governor became alarmed at the absence of Vahíd. He wrote a message to the King saying that he was sure Vahíd had become a follower of the Báb. The King wrote in reply to the governor the following imperial command: "It is strictly forbidden to any one of our subjects to utter such words as would tend to detract from the exalted rank of Vahíd. He is of noble lineage (a Siyyid), a man of great learning, of perfect and consummate virtue. He will under no circumstances incline his ear to any cause unless he believes it to be conducive to the advancement of the best interests of our realm and to the well-being of the Faith of Islam." The King told his prime minister that he had been informed that the famous and renowned Vahíd had become a follower of the Báb and we should stop belittling Him. Upon receipt of this imperial command the governor was unable to harm Vahíd. His face showed its hate and he tried in underhanded ways to hurt him.

Vahíd sent a detailed report of all that happened to the chamberlain of the King for him to give to the King. Vahíd then traveled and taught these new teaching in all parts of Iran.

The Governor in Shiraz was still filled with his hate and envy of the Báb. The Báb's triumphant entry into the city with the governor's troops, the way the Báb had been able to make a public declaration in the Mosque and the way the Báb had won over the King's deputy, Vahíd, infuriated this governor. The governor felt humiliated by the fact that Vahíd had been won over while he was a guest in his own home. Although this governor had put the Báb under house arrest, the Báb had a steady stream of visitors every day to His house of some of the most influential and important people in Iran.

The Báb, knowing what was coming, transferred all of his property to His wife and family, put His worldly affairs in order and moved to the house of His uncle. The governor called his chief of police and told him to take his policemen and late at night open the roof of the uncle's house and arrest everyone there. He was told to bring the Báb to him in handcuffs. The governor declared that very night he would have this Báb executed.

The chief of police with his men made the arrest of the Báb as instructed. In handcuffs they were taking him, in the early morning to the governor's house. The Báb quoted from the Qur'án as He was being arrested, "That with which they are threatened is for the morning. Is not the morning near?"

Suddenly the streets of Shiraz were filled with people in panic and they were fleeing in every direction. The chief of police was told that a plague of the most severe kind had already taken the lives of many people and was sweeping the city with sudden death, just since evening. When they got to the governor's house it was deserted as he had also fled the city. The chief of police then decided to take the Báb to his own home and hold his prisoner there until the governor would return. Upon their arrival at the chief of police's home it was learned that the chiefs son had the plague and was then dying. The chief of police fell on his knees in front of the Báb and begged Him not to punish the son for the sin's of the father. He promised the Báb that if He saved his son, he would quit his job even though he should die of hunger. The Báb had just finished washing His hands and face in preparation for the dawn prayer. He gave him the water he had used and told the chief of police to give it to the boy to drink and the child would live.

As soon as the chief of police saw that his son was indeed going to live, he sent an urgent message to the governor. Pleading that he release the Báb at once, if he did not, no one would be left alive in the city of Shiraz. The governor sent a message back that the Báb was to be released but that He must leave Shiraz at once.

When the King of Iran was duly informed of what had happened he issued an order removing the governor from his post. This ex-governor was deserted by everyone and was even unable to earn his daily bread. Sunk in misery and shame, he languished until his death.

The Báb was unable to return home. From the house of the ex-chief of police, who was now a firm follower of the Báb, his uncle came and in this way He notified His family and He left Shiraz never to see either it or his wife and mother again.

CHAPTER 5
Báb In Isfahan

It was only two years after the Báb's declaration that He was forced to leave forever His home and family. The Báb sent a letter to the Governor of Isfahan before His arrival in the city of Isfahan, asking this governor where he wanted Him to stay. The writing was so beautiful and the language was so respectful and courteous that the Governor went to the highest religious leader of Persia, (Imam) who lived in Isfahan. The Governor requested that this dignitary take care of the Báb. The Imam sent his own brother with a delegation of notables to meet the Báb as He approached Isfahan and accompany Him into the city. The Imam himself went out to welcome the Báb into his own home.

The Báb remained in the house of the Imam for forty days. During His stay there every day and night he was very busy writing and answering all the questions. The fame of the Báb soon spread throughout the city of Isfahan. In those days people used the public baths and after the Báb finished His bath the people of Isfahan would take all the water that He had used for His bath. They claimed that this water cured all their sicknesses.

The Governor, at one of these sessions, asked His Holiness the Báb to prove the truth of

Islam. The Báb instantly took up His pen and in about fifty pages set forth the proof. The Governor was so set on fire by this revelation that he explained to the whole gathering that up to this time in his heart he had not been a confirmed follower of Muhammad. He had many doubts and misgivings and questions that had never been answered. Now he said that after hearing the Báb's explanation that all of his doubts had been explained, all of his questions answered and in the very depths of his heart he now had such certitude in Islam that he was willing to die for it.

The death sentence of the Báb that the Governor in Shiraz had passed, on the night of the plague, had been initiated by the prime minister of the King. Once again this prime minister in Tihrán became alarmed. The prime minister thought that if the King was to meet the Báb that he would lose his high position as the King's spiritual leader and prime minister. When the prime minister began to get reports from Isfahan about this great and mighty Cause, he sent out letters again. He even wrote a letter of condemnation to the Imam. Some of the other clergy, in order to gain favor with the prime minister began a campaign to undermine the popularity of the Báb. The pulpits rang with slander and abuse of the Báb. The governor exerted all his efforts and substantial influence to stem the tide of hate, envy, jealousy and slander.

The governor set up a meeting at his home

and invited all of the most influential clergymen. The purpose of the meeting was to give all these leaders an opportunity to meet His Holiness the Báb and put any questions they might have to him. The governor was sure that the Báb would answer all their questions and in this way stop the attack. Many of the leading clergy refused to attend because they had already been informed of the Báb's supernatural ability and His deepest and most profound knowledge.

The governor after this meeting decided to keep the Báb in his own home in order to better protect Him. At the further instigation of the prime minister the clergy of Isfahan held a conference. They made up a document at that conference condemning the Báb to death. All but two of the participants signed and sealed this warrant. The Imam with whom the Báb had stayed for 40 days, refused to sign it. He however wrote on the document the following testimony: "I testify that in the course of my association with this youth I have been unable to discover any act that would in any way betray his repudiation of the doctrines of Islam. On the contrary I have known him as a pious and loyal observer of its precepts. The extravagance of his claims, however, and his disdainful contempt for the things of the world incline me to believe that he is devoid of reason and judgment." This Imam tried to please both the governor and the manipulated clergy and in the end pleased no one.

The governor was informed of this very cruel, unjust and baseless verdict to put the Báb to death. The governor had it announced that the Báb was requested by the throne to come at once to Tihrán. One evening the governor sent the Báb with five hundred of his own mounted guards out of Isfahan on the road to Tihrán. Then after going for about 6 kilometers, one hundred horsemen returned to Isfahan. After another 6 kilometers another one hundred horsemen of the mounted guards returned to Isfahan. This was repeated until only one hundred guards were left. Then at about each kilometer, twenty horsemen were sent back to Isfahan until only twenty remained. Ten of these the governor instructed to go on to a village and collect the taxes. The remaining ten were the most true and trusted members of the governors guard and they were sworn to secrecy and by an unfrequented route returned the Báb before dawn to Isfahan. The Báb was taken to a side gate of the governor's house and was taken to his private quarters. The Báb remained in the house and a personal guest of the governor for about four more months.

The followers of the Báb were deeply distressed as rumors of His death were circulated. Stories of His suffering, humiliation and defeat were the topic of everyone in the city. Of course the clergy were behind these false reports. They were still trying to undermine the cause and purpose of His Holiness the Báb. Two of the Báb's most trusted friends were brought to the governor's house by the governor and they then shared the news of the Báb's safety to the other friends along with some of His writings not telling anyone where He was.

This governor became a very devoted believer and follower of the Báb. The days that the governor spent with the Báb made him stronger in his faith. One day as they were sitting in the governor's garden. The governor told His Holiness the Báb that God had given him vast wealth and influence. He now planned to use it all for this new and mighty revelation of God. He explained that he planned to go to Tihrán and explain this Cause of God to the king. As a trusted friend and servant of the King, he was sure that he would be able to win his sovereign over to the teachings of the Báb. After that he explained that it was his intention to bring this Most Great Cause of God to the attention of all the Kings and Rulers of the earth. The tender loving heart of the Báb was deeply touched. The Báb then told the governor that because of his pure thoughts and desire God would, in the world to come give to him immortal glory and eternal blessings. However the Báb advised the governor that he only had three months and nine days to live. He also explained to the governor that His Cause and Revelation would one day be accepted by the entire human race and this would come about through the plan of God and was planned by God.

The governor received this news with joy

and started making all the preparations for his departure from this life. The vast wealth of his, he made a will and in his will he left it all to the Báb. The Báb was not at all interested in the things of this world and was well aware of the fact that this desire of His host would never be fulfilled. He explained to the governor that He had the power to change the very stones of the earth into jewels so He had no need of worldly wealth.

The Báb at this time called His two friends and explained what was going to happen in the next few months. He told these friends that they were to get all of His followers in Isfahan to leave Isfahan at once. The above story was circulated among the Bábí s present in Isfahan and as these believers scattered through out Iran the story was spread far and wide long before the governor died.

The nephew of the governor discovered the Báb and advised the King. The King issued the order, ordering the Báb to the capital. This nephew was also commanded to send the Báb in secret with a mounted guard. No one was to know who they were escorting not even the guards themselves. The nephew also stole all the property of his famous and high minded uncle.

In the company of this mounted guard led by Mirza Big they left Isfahan at midnight for Tihrán. This was the last of the Báb's freedom. From that night onward the Báb was a prisoner of the state.

CHAPTER 6
Báb's Journey

Parpa, one of the well known residents of Kashan had a most vivid dream. He dreamt that he was standing at the gate of the city of Kashan in the late afternoon. Suddenly he saw the Báb coming with a mounted guard before and after Him. The Báb greeted him and said, "I am to be your guest for three nights. Prepare to receive me." The Báb was in disguise and was not wearing his customary green turban that indicated His descent from Muhammad.

Parpa set about preparing a feast and then went to the city gate to await the coming arrival of the Báb. This form of communication that so often happened with the Báb was better than our modern Fax and telephone service. What is most amazing is the person having these dreams and visions would respond with assurance that the dream was to take place. As Parpa had dreamt so it happened right up to the exact words of the Báb. This was the third New Years of the Báb's divine revelation. Mirza Big then had a problem with the other officers under his command. The argument that took place was because the mounted guard had received strict orders that the Báb was not to be allowed to enter any city and was not to meet anyone on the trip to Tihrán. The Captain of the guard won out and the

Báb was allowed to accompany Parpa to his home.

The Báb explained to Parpa that all things were held tightly in the Hand of God, and nothing is impossible to Him. He further explained that it was His wish to spend the New Year in peace and quite in the home of Parpa and nothing and no one could stop Him. As the Divine Manifestation of God this power was in His Own Hand. This Parpa became a dedicated and accomplished teacher of the Cause of the Báb. He devoted the rest of his life to this service and although unschooled and unable to read or write he became famous throughout the land.

On the morning of the third day the Báb in keeping with His promise returned to the keeping of Mirza Big and his mounted guards. The journey to Tihrán was continued, but the Báb's love and charm had now won over the entire guard. After another five days of travel they arrived at a place about 30 KM from Tihrán and they expected to reach the capital the next day. A messenger arrived from the capital, issued by the prime minister who was still intent on the destruction of the Báb and his fear of the King falling under the Báb's influence. As the King himself had ordered the Báb to Tihrán the prime minister could not carry out his devilish plan to murder Him. Now the prime minister did the next best thing, he played for time. He ordered the mounted guard to a village that he owned. The prime minister had a tent put up for the Báb and ordered the guard to await further instructions from the King. This country side with its running streams, fresh flowers of spring and the lush vegetation greatly pleased the Báb.

Bahá'u'lláh sent a messenger to the Báb with a sealed letter. This letter brought great joy to the Báb. Then that night the Báb was missing from His tent. The camp was in an uproar and the guards and the Báb's friends that were in the camp set out on the road to Tihrán. They soon saw the lonely figure of the Báb coming from the direction of Tihrán. The thought then as it still is today was did Bahá'u'lláh plan a meeting between Himself and the Báb that night? Did such a meeting actually take place? Bahá'u'lláh never mentioned it. He neither confirmed nor denied having ever met the Blessed Báb that night. We do know from the teachings of both of these Manifestations of God, that they are linked by one and the same Holy Spirit. The eye witnesses of that event all agree that the light and radiance of the Báb seemed to have increased at that point of His journey.

The King sent a personal letter to the Báb which of course had been planned by the fearful prime minister. This prime minister with his bad influence over the King had been the cause of most of the problems that faced the country at that time. The letter was polite in language but was in fact sending the Báb to a very remote area of Persia and into prison in a fortress in the town of Mah-Ku. This town and prison were also owned by this self-seeking prime minister. The mounted guard from Isfahan were instructed to deliver the Báb into the hand of the governor of Tabriz. On this trip to Tabriz two things of importance took place.

Hujjat, a follower of the Báb, had put together a group of people and gave them instructions to rescue the Báb. Some of this group went to the Báb at midnight while all the guards were asleep. The Báb told them to give up their plan as God also had His plan which included His seclusion in the prison of Mah-Ku.

This Mirza Big related as the second event. As they were leaving Milan in the morning a woman came with a child that had been scalded on the head. The burn was covered with scabs and was white to the neck. Mirza Big and his guards were turning the woman and child away when the Báb stopped them. The Báb then put a handkerchief over the child's head and prayed. When the handkerchief was removed the child's head was completely healed. This event was witnessed by over 200 people. Mirza Big and his guard were completely won over by the Báb and His teachings and in Mirza Big's writing referred to the Báb as "The Lord of Mankind".

When they arrived at the city of Tabríz the entire guard went to the Báb, declared their devotion to him and with tears in their eyes asked His forgiveness. This guard then spread the teachings and the great things they had seen to every corner of the land. They turned the Báb over to the heir to the throne who was then the governor of Tabriz.

When the people of Tabríz heard the news of the arrival of the Báb a great turmoil was set into motion. The government sent out an announcement that anyone who tried to meet the Báb would have all of his property taken and would then be put into prison for life. The town criers made this announcement through out the city.

However one of the believers and followers of the Báb, Ali-Askar, along with a merchant went to see Him. They were immediately arrested at the door. The attendant of the Báb came out and told the guards that the Báb had requested these two to come and that He wanted to see them. The guards released the two and they went in to see the Báb. The Báb stated that the guards had been furnished by God to protect Him from the inrush of the people and He would see who ever He wanted and no power on earth could prevent Him. He then gave Ali-Askar two rings to have inscribed. This Ali-Askar had traveled with Mullá Husayn and during their travels had expressed his sadness at never having the opportunity to see the Báb. Mullá Husayn had told him with a firm conviction not to worry that he would in the future, in Tabriz, have seven visits with the Báb. This would be for the one visit that he had missed in Shiraz. Each time Ali-Askar came to talk about the inscription he was admitted without question and on the seventh visit he was amazed when the Báb said. "Thank God that you have been blessed with your seven promised visits."

The Báb remained in Tabríz for forty days. Then one day his attendant asked him if they were going to stay in Tabriz. The Báb told his attendant that they would spend 9 months in Mah-Ku and then they would be transferred to Chihrig. Five days latter they were sent to Mah-Ku just as the Báb had predicted. They were delivered into the hands of a relative of the prime minister named Ali Khan the warden of the castle. This castle was on a mountain over looking the town of Mah-Ku. Ali Khan was given strict orders that no one, absolutely no one was to be allowed to see the Báb. Ali Khan was severe in his duty and when a follower of the Báb would arrive in Mah-Ku town he would not even allow them to stay in town, not even over night.

One day when the Báb had been informed that there was a follower outside the town gate, He told his attendant when he went into the town the next day to tell this believer that on the following day Ali-Khan would come and get him and would bring him to the Báb. The attendant and the believer could not imagine this stiff necked ,severe and unbending warden would change.

Early the following morning the attendant was surprised by a sudden knock on the door. As it was before sunrise and the rule of the warden was that absolutely no one was to be admitted before sunrise. The warden Ali Khan came into the room of the Báb and his character was completely changed. He stood in the door with an attitude of humility, his self assurance was gone.

What had happened was early that morning as the warden was riding towards the town of Mah-Ku he saw the Báb standing by the side of the river saying His prayers. He started towards the Báb to get Him and bring Him back to the castle. As the warden drew near he was overcome by the extreme devotion and rapture of the Báb as He said His prayers. He was still determined to interrupt the Báb, but suddenly he was filled with a great fear. Ali Khan then decided to scold the guards for having let the Báb out. So he rode directly to the castle and found both the outer and inner gates locked. Then to his utter amazement he discovered the Báb here in His room. The Warden threw himself at the feet of the Báb and begged His forgiveness. The Báb explained that prison walls were powerless to contain the light of God. Ali Khan was instantly converted to the cause of the Báb. He begged the Báb to let him go personally and conduct the believer that was outside the gate in to see Him.

Ali Khan became an ardent follower of the Báb and did everything in his power to make up for his past severe treatment of God's Holy Manifestation.

Those that made the long and difficult

journey to visit the Báb were rewarded by being able to visit Him. This confinement now gave the Báb time and peace and over one hundred thousand verses were revealed at this time and distributed throughout the land by the constant stream of visitors that poured in from every place. He also revealed the Persian Bayan at this time. This book is the same as the Scriptures of Jesus for the Christians and the Qur'án for the Muslims. The primary theme of all these writings was about the coming of Bahá'u'lláh

The people of Mah-Ku were so won over by the Báb that every day before they went to their daily work they would come to the castle and seek His blessing. When they had any disputes they would come to the castle and stand beneath His window and then demand that in the presence of the Lord of the world they should speak only the truth.

In the meantime Mullá Husayn had determined to make a pilgrimage to Mah-Ku to visit the Báb. Mullá Husayn was then in Mashad. Mashad is a city in the northeast corner of Iran and Mah-Ku is in the extreme northwest corner a distance of about fifteen hundred kilometers. Mullá Husayn decided to walk the whole distance as a tribute to his great love and devotion to His Holiness the Báb. Mullá Husayn left Mashad in the middle of the night with only one attendant. When the followers of the Báb discovered that Mullá Husayn had left they went after him and offered him horses and expenses and many wanted to go with him. To everything he refused and they were turned back to Mashad.

In every town through which Mullá Husayn passed he was met by an enthusiastic crowd. All these believers were touched by his spirit and their faith in His holiness the Báb was through him made stronger. When he came to Tihrán he was the guest of Bahá'u'lláh and this blessing further strengthen the fire of love that had inflamed his heart and soul.

The night before the arrival of Mullá Husayn at the castle of Mah-Ku, Ali Khan the warden had a dream. He dreamed that the next day the Prophet of God, Muhammad, was going to arrive at Mah-Ku and would celebrate the fourth new year of this new revelation with the Báb. In his dream Ali Khan rushed out to the road leading into Mah-Ku and in the distance he saw two men coming. The one in the lead he recognized to be the Prophet Himself. Ali Khan rushed forward and was bowing to the feet of the Prophet when he awoke. The following account was recorded in the words of Ali Khan:

"A great joy had flooded my soul. I felt as if Paradise itself, with all its delights, had been crowded into my heart. Convinced of the reality of my vision, I bathed, offered my prayer, put on my best and finest clothes, perfumed myself and went to the place on the road I had seen in my dream and where I had seen the Prophet of God. I had ordered my servants to saddle three of my best horses and bring them to me. The sun had just risen when alone and unescorted, I walked out of the town of Mah-Ku in the direction of the river. As I approached the bridge, I discovered, with a throb of wonder, the two men whom I had seen in my dream coming towards me. Instinctively I fell at the feet of the one whom I believed to be the Prophet, devoutly kissed them. I begged Him and His companion to mount the horses which I had prepared for their entry into Mah-Ku. 'No,' was His reply, 'I have vowed to accomplish this whole journey on foot, I will walk to the summit of this mountain and will there visit your Prisoner'"

This strange and wonderful experience had a profound effect on Ali Khan. His faith was deepened and his love, respect and devotion to the Báb was increased. The Báb met Mullá Husayn at the gate of the castle with a loving embrace and together they celebrated the fourth new year celebration. The food that Ali Khan had brought was the most delicious and the Báb called it the feast in the Land of Paradise.

The Báb informed Mullá Husayn that His time in Mah-Ku was now over. Mullá Husayn was advised by the Báb of His transfer to another mountain in the near future. In fact the prime minister was receiving reports of Mah-Ku and the change, transformation and conversion of his trusted relative the warden Ali Khan to the Cause of the Báb. Mullá Husayn stayed with the Báb in Mah-Ku for nine days. He was advised by the Báb the cities he was to visit and his destination was to be the province of Mazindaran. He was instructed by His Holiness the Báb to return as he had come, that is on foot and he was further advised that Mullá Husayn's days of horsemanship was in the future. He was told that he would be called upon in the future to demonstrate such skill and heroism that would eclipse the mightiest deeds of the heros of old. The parting instruction from the Báb to his first believer, Mullá Husayn, was to convey the love of the Báb to all His followers and was to inflame their hearts with the love of Bahá'u'lláh and prepare them for His revelation. When Mullá Husayn was to reach Mazindaran he would find a hidden treasure that God would show to him.

Twenty days after the New Year the Báb was moved to Chihriq. The prime minister of the King was still filled with fear of the Báb. The Báb's fame and teachings were in fact growing across Persia at an alarming rate. The prime minister's plot, by removing the Báb to Mah-Ku, actually helped His Divine Cause to grow by giving the Báb time and place for writing. The Báb had been in Mah-Ku for nine months when He was transferred to Chihríq.

CHAPTER 7
Mullá Husayn

Mullá Husayn, faithful to the Báb's instructions, visited all the towns and cities he had been told to, and once again in Tihrán visited Bahá'u'lláh. He then traveled still on foot to the Province of Mazindaran, where the Báb had told him he would discover a hidden treasure. He went directly to the home of Quddús. A big dinner had been prepared in honor of Mullá Husayn and many friends had been invited. The guests were amazed at the high honor that Quddús showed to Mullá Husayn. After the dinner and the departure of the guests, Quddús questioned Mullá Husayn about the instructions he had received from the Báb.

When Mullá Husayn explained about the hidden treasure that he was to find in Mazindaran, Quddús gave Mullá Husayn a book that he had written. Mullá Husayn read only the first page and he immediately arose from his seat of honor. He crossed the room to the door and in an attitude of complete humility said, "The hidden treasure of which the Báb has spoken, now lies unveiled before my eyes. Though my Master be now hidden (a prisoner in Chihriq). . .I have found in Mazindaran the reflection of His glory."

The foolish prime minister of Persia had mistakenly thought that he could hide the Light of God. What in fact he had succeeded in doing, was to put the Light of God upon a mountain top where its light, fire and brilliance radiated out in all directions. That Light and Fire which would eventually illuminate the whole world.

Mullá Husayn, was a saint, a holy man, an angel and will be an example for man to try and follow for thousands of years. His instant, exact and complete self sacrificing obedience was sincere and profound. His instant recognition of the Báb before anyone else. His complete submission to the will of God when Quddús had been chosen instead of Mullá Husayn, to travel with His Holiness the Báb to Mecca and Medina. Now with Mullá Husayn's own vast knowledge and his superior position and the great esteem and love of the Báb's followers, he once again showed his greatness and self-sacrificing spirit in bowing to the will of God as reflected in the person of Quddús.

Quddús sent Mullá Husayn on to the next province with instructions to prepare an institute building and to invite all the followers of the Báb to come to this institute. There Quddús and Mullá Husayn would prepare them as a teaching team to teach and proclaim this new and wondrous word of God.

In the area of Mashad, a property was found and adequate quarters were built. Upon the completion of the building Quddús arrived and the classes were started. A steady stream of believers arrived and were prepared by Mullá Husayn and taught by Quddús. These classes were spiritual transformation classes and the people that attended were set on fire by the love and spirit of the teachings of His Holiness the Báb.

Chapter 8
The Báb in Chihriq

The warden of the castle of C̱hihríq whose sister was one of the wives of the King was informed by the prime minister not to fall victim to his prisoner's charm. This warden was informed of the conversion of Ali Khan of Mah-ku to the teachings of the Báb. This warden was given the most strict orders to keep the Báb in absolute isolation and that no one was to be permitted to see Him. In spite of this strong order issued by the prime minister the warden of Chihriq, from his first meeting with the Báb, was so moved that his very soul was set on fire with love for the Báb and His teachings, that everyone who came to the castle of C̱hihríq was allowed to see Him. In fact the castle of C̱hihríq was unable to accommodate the huge throng of people that came to visit the Báb and had to be lodged an hour's distance away.

A very high official who had openly and privately denounced the Báb and His teachings had a dream. When he woke up he did not tell anyone about it. He then took the Qur'án and chose two verses and then wrote a letter to the Báb. In the letter he said, "I have three definite things in my mind. I request you to reveal to me their nature." When he received a reply written by the Báb. The Báb explained the dream in detail and wrote in detail what he had in his mind. When this official received this revelation he went all the way to Chihríq on foot and presented himself to the Báb. With this confirmation he started in teaching the God inspired teachings of His Holiness the Báb.

This official by the name of Dayyan was a firm and staunch follower of the Báb to the end of his life. Dayyan's father was very upset and being a friend of the prime minister, he wrote him a letter complaining about his son and the conversion of the warden of the castle. He also informed the prime minister of the great number of high and important people that were won over to the cause of the Báb. About this time also a holy man from India who had been won over through his spiritual insight had walked all the way from India to Chihríq to visit the Báb.

When this news was sent to the central government along with various reports an order was issued to transfer the Báb at once to Tabriz. Before this order was issued the Báb had sent all of the friends away.

In one of the towns where the Báb stopped on His journey to Tabríz He was the guest of a prince. In order to test the Báb this prince ordered his groom to saddle up a very wild horse. This horse had thrown the most skillful and bravest horsemen. Everyone in the town knew of this wild and untamed horse. The groom, who was very much attracted to the Báb, went to the Báb in secret and told Him not to try to mount the horse as He could be seriously injured. The Báb told the groom to not be afraid and to do as the prince had commanded.

This news of the wild horse and the Báb's forthcoming ride spread throughout the town. Everyone turned out to see the show. The Báb was going to the bath and the wild horse was brought for Him to ride. The Báb quietly approached the horse and mounted. The horse stood very quiet and motionless. The Báb rode to the bath and afterwards returned to His quarters on the same animal. The people of that town carried away all the water from the bath, certain that because the Báb had bathed in it, that this water would cure all their ills.

The news of the Báb's arrival in Tabríz spread like wildfire through the city. The entire population was in a state of frenzied excitement. The fame and enthusiasm for the Báb swept over Persia and engulfed the capital of Tihrán. The prime minister issued urgent orders to the leaders of Tabríz to extinguish at all costs the influence of the Báb. A meeting of all the religious and government leaders was speedily arranged and even the crown prince was in attendance.

The Báb entered the hall and as all the seats were occupied, He went with dignity and a sense of majesty to the seat reserved for the crown prince and sat down. Such a spirit of power was felt from His divine presence that a deep and mysterious silence settled over the meeting hall. When the chairman of the meeting asked the Báb who He claimed to be, the Báb replied in a ringing and majestic voice: **"I AM, I AM, I AM THE PROMISED ONE!** I am the One whose name you have for a thousand years invoked, at whose mention you have risen, whose advent you have longed to witness, and the hour of whose Revelation you have prayed God to hasten."

Immediately after He had declared Himself to be the promised One, a feeling of awe seized those who were present. They had dropped their heads in silent confusion. The pallor of their faces betrayed the agitation of their hearts. When the leaders regained their composure they began to bring up frivolous and senseless points. The Báb answered by saying, "I maintain what I have already declared." When they continued their discussion on the rules of grammar, the Báb got up and with the same dignity and majesty walked out.

The leaders of Tabríz decided to punish the Báb for taking the seat of the crown prince and for leaving the meeting without permission from the chairman. They decreed that the Báb should receive a beating on the soles of His feet. The guard refused to do this and so one of the high priests applied the rod 11 times to the Báb's feet and also stuck Him in the face.

That same year this high priest was struck with paralysis, and in the most excruciating pain died a miserable death. He was abandoned, and hated by everyone.

The Báb was returned to Chihríq. This challenging declaration made by the Báb swept across Persia and as far away as Iraq. The government and religious leaders had greatly miscalculated. All that meeting did was to give the Báb greater importance and completely frustrate the purpose of these leaders to humiliate in public His Holiness the Báb.

Chapter 9
Fort Tabarsi

Mullá Husayn was still in Mashad conducting the spiritual transformation classes. Quddús had attended a meeting with Bahá'u'lláh and the renowned Táhirih. After the meeting Quddús was taken prisoner and was confined in the town of Sari in Mazindaran. At this time Mullá Husayn received a message and package from the Báb. He was told to put on the enclosed green turban of the Báb, unfurl the black standard and go help Quddús.

The Prophet of God Muhammad had said, "Should your eyes behold the Black Standards proceeding from Khurasan, hasten ye towards them, even though ye should have to crawl over the snow, inasmuch as they proclaim the advent of the promised Mihdi (Manifestation)."

With 202 devoted followers, on July 21, 1884 about 2.5 KM from Mashad, on the road to Mazindaran in the province of Khurasan the black standard, (promised by Muhammad) was raised. The green turban worn by Mullá Husayn was a sign of the descendant of Muhammad and was also foretold by Muhammad that in the last days the loved ones of God would be led into Mazindaran by one wearing the green turban.

In each city, town, village and hamlet that this group passed through they would stop and proclaim the new message of God that had been manifested by the Báb. Also they gained new recruits as they made their way to Mazindaran. On September 4, 1848 as they paused to rest a strong gale of wind broke a branch off of a tree. Mullá Husayn explained that the tree of the King had been uprooted and hurled to the ground. On the third day after this event news was received that the King had died on September 4. 1848.

As the little band of Mullá Husayn's was some little distance from the city of Barfurùsh, (this city today is called Bábul), the high priest of the city had a town crier go through out the city and invite all the people to a meeting. At this meeting this high priest tore open his shirt, threw his turban to the ground and worked the population into a frenzy about Mullá Husayn and his group now moving towards their city. He shouted and screamed about Mullá Husayn being from Satan and that he was intent on uprooting the Faith of Islam. He demanded that the people all together go forth and kill these enemies of Muhammad. He further declared this to be a holy war and by obeying his command they would be certain to attain unto paradise. He thundered on that if they refused to obey him, all their property would be plundered by Mullá Husayn and his followers. He ranted on about how this was the duty of the young and old, the women and the men to arm themselves and the next morning at dawn to go forth and kill this entire company of Mullá Husayn's.

The entire population arose to his call, because this high priest held the highest position in the city, his supposed knowledge of the Holy Qur'án and the fear of losing lives and property. They armed themselves with guns, knives clubs and any weapon they could find and started out.

Mullá Husayn guided by the Hand of Providence told his companions to throw everything they owned onto the side of the road keeping only their horses and swords. He also warned them that in the future they would be unable to leave and if anyone felt unable to sustain the trials that lay ahead they should leave at once. About 20 out of the 202 left at that time.

About 2Km from the city Mullá Husayn and his tiny band were met by this hostile and armed band. These followers of Mullá Husayn started to take out their swords. Mullá Husayn stopped them telling the group that not until they were attacked must they attempt to defend themselves. Immediately six of them were shot down and then another one was shot down. Mullá Husayn raised his eyes to heaven and declared that God knew that their only desire was to guide people to the teachings of God and that God had also commanded them to defend themselves. Mullá Husayn then took out his sword and rushed into the midst of the enemy. He went after the one who had fired the seventh shot. This man tried to defend himself by hiding behind his gun and a tree. With one super human effort, Mullá Husayn cut through the tree, the gun and the man. When the people of Barfurùsh witnessed this they all fled in a panic. This feat was verified by both the companions of Mullá Husayn and the enemies of Barfurùsh. When Quddús was informed of this he quoted the Qur'án, "So it was not ye who slew them but God who slew them;"

Mullá Husayn then rode on alone right into the city and to the home of the high priest. As he circled around that house on his horse he proclaimed, "Let that contemptible coward who has incited the inhabitants of this town to wage holy warfare against us and has hid himself in his house come forth and as commanded in the Qur'án that the one who wages a holy war needs to lead that war in the front of battle." The inhabitants of the city cried out peace, peace which Mullá Husayn instantly granted. The companions of Mullá Husayn came thundering in on their horses shouting "O Thou Lord of the Age!"

Mullá Husayn and his group then went to a youth house in the city. The people of Barfurùsh instigated further by the high priest decided to break the peace. When it was time to call the faithful to evening prayer, Mullá Husayn asked for a volunteer to go on to the roof of the youth house and sacrifice his life by calling the faithful to prayer. A young man arose and had no sooner said the opening lines of the prayer than he was shot dead. Another volunteered and met the same fate and the third one as he finished the call to prayer was killed. Mullá Husayn and his friends mounted their horses and rushed upon their enemies. The city center was filled with an angry, seething mob intent on killing Mullá Husayn and his friends. For the second time the cry of "O Thou Lord of the age!" was raised and soon the entire square was deserted except for the dead. Once again the leaders of Barfurùsh cried for mercy and peace and once again Mullá Husayn granted it.

The leaders and notables of Barfarush came to Mullá Husayn and brought with them a Qur'án on which they swore that they would not again take up arms against him. They ordered a captain and a hundred horsemen to accompany Mullá Husayn and his company the next morning and insure their safety along the way. The high priest during the night called the captain of the guard that had been assigned to see Mullá Husayn and his followers on their way. This high priest instructed the captain that he was to take them by an unfrequented road and when they got into the forest, him and his men were to kill Mullá Husayn and all of his companions. The captain of the guard argued with the high priest and said that everyone knew that these men would rather die than miss saying their call to prayer. The high priest got very angry and said that he was the authority and he would personally answer to God on the day of judgment. He further declared that he as high priest was in a better position to know the truth than a captain of the guard.

The next morning they departed with the captain of the guard and his one hundred horsemen. At the hour of noon Mullá Husayn stopped to say his mid day prayer. In the middle of the prayer the cry of "O Thou Lord of the age!" was once again raised when the companions of Mullá Husayn were attacked. The captain of the guard and his horsemen all died in that attack. Only one of the attendants who begged for mercy was spared. He was given his captains water pipe and told to report all that happened to the leaders of Barfarush.

The Báb from His prison in Chihríq had issued orders to the Bábís (followers of the Báb) to go at once to Mazindaran and help Mullá Husayn. This instruction had been sent out upon the Báb's return from Tabriz. This was around the end of August in 1848. The Bábís with Mullá Husayn had their first skirmish with the mob from Barfurùsh on October 10, 1848 and had defended themselves against the guard that had attempted to murder them on October 11, 1848. About 20 Km south east of Barfurùsh there was a small shrine called Shaykh Tabarsí named after one of the followers of Shaykh Ahmad. When Mullá Husayn arrived with his band at this spot they were once again set upon by a savage mob and once again raised their battle cry of

"O Thou Lord of the age!" jumped to their horses and sent the mob fleeing in every direction. Mullá Husayn decided to fortify the shrine of Tabarsí and the Bábís all turned to with a will.

Now it might be supposed by the valor and spirit of the Bábís that they were all trained soldiers. This was not the case. The entire party was made up of students, merchants and ordinary people untrained in the art of warfare. When the gun, the tree, and the man that had been cut into six pieces by one stroke of Mullá Husayn's sword and the six pieces were shown around. It was reported that Mullá Husayn had been trained in the art of swordsmanship from childhood. The family and friends that had known Mullá Husayn all his life said that this was a lie. Mullá Husayn had been a student and had spent all his time in the study of religion. The title Mulla in English means a priest. His close friend explained that Mullá Husayn was so weak that he could not even write for an extended period without becoming exhausted. Mullá Husayn was completely transformed when he put on the green turban of the Báb and raised the black standard. All those who knew him verified that he was filled with the spirit of God and no one could stand against him from that time onward.

The night before the Bábís arrival at Tabarsí the guardian of the shrine dreamed that the next day the Holy Imam would arrive with a group of followers and great and heroic deeds were to take place at his shrine. When Mullá Husayn did arrive the next day the guardian of the shrine recognized him and became one of the devoted Bábís.

The fortification of Tabarsí had just been completed when the news came that Bahá'u'lláh was coming. Mullá Husayn, himself helped with the sprinkling and sweeping of the approaches to the fort. As soon as Mullá Husayn saw Bahá'u'lláh he rushed forward and embraced Him. He introduced Bahá'u'lláh with love and reverence to the others. Mullá Husayn was so captivated by his love for Bahá'u'lláh that he left everyone standing and it was Bahá'u'lláh who finally told them to be seated. Bahá'u'lláh inspected the fort and then told Mullá Husayn to send seven men to the town of Sari where Quddús was being held a prisoner and demand his release. He informed Mullá Husayn that with the arrival of Quddús to take command of the fort all would be perfect. Bahá'u'lláh said as He left Tabarsi, "You have been chosen of God to be the vanguard of His host and the establisher of His Faith. His host verily will conquer. Whatever may befall, victory is yours, a victory which is complete and certain."

Mullá Husayn immediately sent the seven horsemen to Sari and the high priest of Sari delivered up Quddús as Bahá'u'lláh had said he would. Quddús had been a prisoner in Sari for ninety five days. Upon the arrival of Quddús one of the first things he did was to take a count of the

Bábís in the fort. The count was three hundred and twelve and just as Mullá Husayn was going to report to Quddús a youth from Barfurúsh rushed in and the count was exactly three hundred and thirteen. In the traditions of Muhammad it is said, "And when the Manifestation is made manifest, He shall lean His back against the Holy place and shall address to the three hundred and thirteen followers who will have grouped around Him, these words, 'The Remnant of God will be best for you if ye are of those who believe.'" Quddús quoted this tradition as he dismounted from his horse and he pointed out that the Remnant of God meant Bahá'u'lláh.

The high priest of Barfurúsh sent an urgent letter to the new King about the fort and asked for help. Náiri'd-Din Sháh who had been a participant as crown prince in Tabarsí when the Báb openly declared who He was, was inexperienced and so turned the matter over to his military advisors. One of these advisors was from Mazindaran and he informed the King saying, "The handful of untrained and frail-bodied students whom I have seen are utterly powerless to withstand the forces which your majesty can command." So the King issued a decree and sent with it a royal badge. An army of about twelve thousand soldiers were dispatched to Tabarsí to put down what the government called a rebellion. The expectation was that two days would see the rebellion finished.

This army set up its camp near the fort and

constructed a number of barricades. The orders were to shoot anyone who came or went to the fort. All water and food that was being supplied from outside was in this way cut off. One of the Bábís asked Quddús what were they to do. Quddús explained that tonight we will have all the water we require, and this rain will be followed by a heavy snow fall that will relieve our situation.

That night the army was surprised by a torrential rain that not only drenched the camp but destroyed most of the powder and ammunition. The following night a record snowfall brought desolation to the camp of the army and a much needed relief to the Bábís in the fort. Enough water was stored to last them for a long time. This was on December 1, 1848. The night after the snow storm Quddús and Mullá Husayn with the three hundred and thirteen followers left the fort and once again the cry of "O Thou Lord of the age!" was raised by the Bábís. This cry shouted in unison echoed across the countryside. It stunned the soldiers of the army and most of them ran off in every direction. All the officers of the army were slain along with four hundred and thirty of their men. None of the Bábís were killed and only one man was wounded. The Bábís were commanded by Quddús not to take any of the property and he ordered them all to return to the fort. Quddús explained that having routed the army, that was enough and their purpose was to defend themselves only and they must continue their work for the regeneration of men.

A new army was dispatched headed by a prince this time, three regiments of infantry, several regiments of cavalry and cannons were brought to a place overlooking the fort. The command had been issued to bombard the fort. It was still dark when the Bábís once more pealed out "O Thou Lord of the age!" and two hundred and two of them rushed into the camp of the army. Mullá Husayn rushed into the apartments of the prince and this prince, fearing for his life, jumped out of the window and bare footed ran into the forest. Two other princes of royal blood were killed. In the apartments of these princes they found cases of gold and valuables which they did not touch. In the course of the battle the army of the prince cut off a small group of Bábís and Quddús was wounded in the mouth. When Mullá Husayn arrived, with a sword in each hand he routed the rest of the prince's army. The entire battle lasted only thirty minutes. This battle took place on December 21, 1848.

Bahá'u'lláh, who was on His way back to Tabarsí to help was taken prisoner in Amul, along with several of His companions. The governor of Amul was absent serving in the army of the prince at Tabarsí. The acting governor in order to appease the clergy that wanted them killed had Bahá'u'lláh beaten on the feet. This punishment was the same as the one inflicted upon the Báb in Tabriz. He then succeeded in transferring Bahá'u'lláh to his own house. Bahá'u'lláh was kept in strict confinement in that house until the Governor returned from Tabarsi.

This governor of Amul had been completely changed. He had gone off to Tabarsí intent on the destruction of the Bábís. He had returned after witnessing the holy spiritual atmosphere of the Bábís compared with the drunkenness, gambling and women that he had seen in the army camp. He was now convinced that if anyone was from God it was the defenders at Tabarsí. He went directly to Bahá'u'lláh and apologized to Him for the bad treatment He had received. The governor prepared for the return of Bahá'u'lláh and His companions to Tihrán.

The army was constantly being reinforced and they had constructed seven barricades. The Bábís in the fort had just dug a well and Mullá Husayn bathed, put on new clothes and cleansed of all earthly things, indicated that he would now seek the court of the Almighty. The cry of "O Thou Lord of the age!' again went up this time so powerful that it resounded through the forest, fort and camp.

Mulla Husyan and his companions broke through the first barricade which was defended by the enemies most valiant officer. Then, with the same force, demolished the remaining six barricades. One of the enemy had climbed a tree and shot Mullá Husayn. Mullá Husayn got off of his horse, bleeding and staggered a few steps and collapsed. He was carried back to the fort bleeding and unconscious and taken to Quddús. Quddús told everyone to leave him alone with Mullá Husayn. One of the friends stated that he watched through a crack. As soon as Quddús called out Mullá Husayn's name. Mullá Husayn got up and knelt in his customary position in front of Quddús. Quddús talked with Mullá Husayn for about two hours. He then called the attendants and they found Mullá Husayn dead with a smile on his face. Mullá Husayn was laid to rest in the shrine of Shakyh Tabarsí along with the thirty six Bábís that died that night. He was just thirty six years old. Bahá'u'lláh in His Book of Certitude made the following statement about Mullá Husayn:

"Among them was Mullá Husayn, who became the recipient of the effulgent glory of the Sun of divine Revelation. But for him, God would not have been established upon the seat of His mercy, nor ascended the throne of eternal glory."

Mullá Husayn was taken to his heavenly homeland February 2, 1849. The great historian of these events wrote, "In each encounter he distinguished himself by such acts of valor, of chivalry, of skill, and of strength that each one would alone suffice to establish for all time the transcendent character of a Faith for the protection of which he had so valiantly fought, and in the path of which he had so nobly died. The traits of mind and or character which, from his very youth, he displayed, the profundity of his leaning, the tenacity of his Faith, his intrepid courage, his singleness of purpose, his high sense of justice and unswerving devotion, marked him as an outstanding figure among those who, by their lives, have borne witness to the glory and power of the new Revelation."

The camp of the army was in disarray and for forty five days they just tried to reassemble their forces. The army did not know of the death of Mullá Husayn. The Bábís were reduced to eating the grass from the field and they even ground up the bones of the dead horses to eat. They boiled the leather from the saddles for what little nourishment it could give. Quddús assembled all the Bábís and instructed them that anyone who wanted must leave. That very night one of the companions of Quddús betrayed them. He wrote a note to the general of the army and explained that Mullá Husayn was dead and that he could now take the fort with no opposition. Another person stole out of the fort after midnight and delivered the message to the general. The general was demoralized and was thinking of returning to Tihrán or thinking of going home when the messenger came. This news renewed his courage and he killed the messenger so that no one else would know of the death of Mullá Husayn. The general assembled his forces and marching at the head of two regiments attacked the fort from all sides. Quddús sent out only eighteen Bábís this time with the assurance that the power they possessed was of God and although Mullá Husayn was gone that power was still with them. "O Thou Lord of the age!" sent chills of fear through the army and they ran away in all directions. The general fell off of his horse and ran after the army leaving one of his boots in the stirrup of the saddle.

Another general took over the army and sent to the capital for reinforcements, bomb shells and camel-artillery. The famished Bábís in the fort were receiving daily their inspiration from Quddús and their spirits and moral was very high. Night and day the soldiers outside the fort could hear the Bábís singing their praises and thanksgiving to God. These songs seemed to sap the soldiers vitality and strength. In their hearts they knew that they were fighting against the power of God. The Bahá'í new year on March 21, 1849 was spent in prayer inside the fort.

With the new bomb shells and artillery the bombardment of the fort continued and the soldiers were amazed that the singing and prayers still issued from the fort. Quddús told the Bábís in the fort that each one of them had an appointed hour and this entire engagement had been foretold in the Holy Qur'án. Neither the assault of the enemy nor the help of their friends could advance or retard that hour. All men must live and one day die. Where were the Kings and Rulers of the past? They are all gone and for the most part forgotten. At least these pure hearted men when they died, would have given their lives for truth, honor, virtue and to improve the lives of all future generations by leading their children's children not only by words but by example in obedience to God.

The army then constructed four towers that commanded a view into the heart of the fort. With their artillery from these towers the effects would be deadly. So once again the gate of the fort was thrown open and eighteen Bábís and their leader sounded their dreaded, "O Thou Lord of the Age!" and were able to destroy all these towers and throw their guns to the ground. All nineteen of the Bábís returned safely to the fort.

Never since the beginning of this contest had the Bábís ever gone on the offensive. When attacked they most fiercely defended themselves and when the enemy had been humiliated and routed, they never pressed their advantage, but instead returned to their prayers and their fort. They never even took away any of the possessions of the army even sorely needed supplies. Their trust and confidence in God as the best and only helper was sufficient for them.

April 24, 1849 the bombardment of the fort was made stronger and once more the army, with a number of officers and cavalry advanced toward the fort. This time only thirty six Bábís flung open the gate and raising that fearful cry rushed into the fray. The same fear and consternation disseminated the army and they fled away. Five of the thirty six were killed during this last engagement.

It seems unbelievable that eighteen or thirty six or the entire three hundred and thirteen could defeat an army in excess of twelve thousand trained soldiers. This, however was a historical fact that was witnessed by both Bahá'í witnesses to the battle and other historians of the day that were able to leave no doubt as to the truth of the matter.

A messenger arrived from the King with a royal decree. This messenger was allowed to approach the fort and as he had a personal friend in the fort, he asked to speak to him. The following was the report of that messenger:

"I saw Mulla Mihdi appear above the wall of the fort, his face wore an expression of stern resolve that baffled description. He looked as fierce as a lion, his sword was fastened over a long white shirt after the manner of the Arabs, and he had a white kerchief around his head. 'What is it that you seek? Say it quickly, for I fear that my master will summon me and find me absent.' The determination that glowed in his eyes confused me. I was dumbfounded at his looks and manner. The thought suddenly flashed through my mind that I would awaken a dormant sentiment in his heart. I reminded him of his infant child, Rahman (merciful), whom he had left behind in the village, in his eagerness to enlist under the black standard of Mullá Husayn. In his love for this child he had written a song which he would sing as he rocked the child to sleep in his crib. 'Your beloved Rahman longs for you and the love you once showered upon him. The baby is alone and needs you.' 'Tell him for me that the love of the true Rahman, a love that transcends all earthly affections, has so filled my heart that it has left no place for any other love besides His.' The force and conviction of his words brought tears to my eyes. I cursed those who considered him and the other Bábís to have strayed from the true path of God.

'What,' I asked him, 'if I venture to enter the fort and join you?' 'If your motive be to seek and find the truth,' he calmly replied, 'I will gladly show you the way. And if you seek to visit me as an old and lifelong friend, I will accord you the welcome of which the Prophet of God, Muhammad has spoken: "Welcome your guests though they be of the infidels." I will be faithful to that command, offer you the boiled grass and churned bones which serve as my food, the very best that I have. If your intention is to harm me, I warn you that I will defend myself and hurl you from this wall to the ground.' I was convinced that all the Kings and the wealth of the earth would never get him to leave the Beloved of his heart, or the path to God that he had found. I then told him of the decree of the King and the assurances of the prince in charge of the army.

'The prince has vowed that anyone who will leave the fort now will be guaranteed safety and his expenses paid back to his home.' I explained."

A few of the participants upon receiving the message about their guaranteed safety left the fort and were instantly put to death by the general of the army.

On May 9, 1849 the prince and his generals sent a message to the fort requesting negotiations which of course Quddús allowed and sent two Bábís. The Prince took a copy of the Holy Qur'án and wrote on the margin of the first page. "I swear by this most Holy Book, by the righteousness of God who has revealed it, and the Mission of Him who was inspired with its verses, that I cherish no other purpose than to promote peace and friendliness between us. Come out of your fort and be assured that no hand will be stretched forth against you, You, yourself and your companions, I solemnly declare, are under the sheltering protection of the Almighty, of Muhammad, His Prophet and of Náiri'd-Din Sháh , our King. I pledge my honor that no man, either in this army or in this neighborhood, will ever attempt to harm you. The malediction of God, the omnipotent Avenger, rest upon me if in my heart I cherish any other desire than that which I have stated." He then signed it and put his seal on it.

Quddús received the Qur'án and kissed it. He knew that the army was not sincere, but he told the Bábís that they would leave the fort. Of the three hundred and thirteen who had gone into the fort only two hundred and two came out. The black standard that had been hoisted on July 3, 1848 and had waved over the fort of Tabarsi, as foretold by Muhammad over a thousand years before now came down. The prince and generals had put up a tent where the Bábís went. Quddús told his companions that during the night they should all slip away as they would surely be put to death. They all refused to leave Quddús and would rather be killed than leave him.

    The next day, as Quddús had foretold, the Bábís were all put to death except for a few that were sold into slavery. These few were spared by the Hand of God to report the entire story to the children yet to be born. Quddús was taken into his home town of Barfurùsh and was taken in chains through the city where all of the people with knives and spears and stones attacked him and tore his body to pieces and threw the pieces into the fire. This story of Tabarsi, brought about the conversion of thousands of people to the Cause of the Báb and proclaimed his message far and wide.

Chapter 10
Darkness before Dawn

The scene now shifts to Tihrán the capital. The time was March 15, 1850. Seven of the most popular people in Persia that had accepted the teachings of the Báb were put death. Their only crime being that they believed the Báb to be a divine manifestation of God. The first was the renowned merchant from Shiraz the maternal uncle of the Báb and the one who had cared for the Báb from His infancy. When questioned and told to deny the Báb and he would be freed he said, " To refuse to acknowledge the Mission of the Báb would be to reject the faith of my forefathers and to deny the Divine Message which Moses, Jesus, Muhammad and all the Prophets have taught. God knows that whatever I have heard and read concerning the sayings and doings of those Messengers, I have been privileged to witness the same from the Báb, this beloved Kinsman of mine, from His earliest boyhood to this, the thirtieth year of His life."

Several of those seven that were killed at that time held the station of high priests. They all refused to deny the station of the Báb and declared that to do so would be to deny all the Holy Souls of the past and Messengers and Prophets of God.

The man the King had sent to Shiraz to investigate and had become a devoted follower of the Báb as a result of his three interviews, was Vahíd. He traveled and taught the new teachings with openness and vigor. As he had memorized the Qur'án and thousands of traditions he was able to back up his teachings so that anyone whom he met, if they were fair and open minded, accepted the teachings of the Báb. Vahíd spent a great deal of time with Bahá'u'lláh in Tihrán. This time spent with Bahá'u'lláh further inspired him. He was on his way to join Mullá Husayn when Bahá'u'lláh returned to Tihrán and informed him that it was impossible to get to Tabarsi.

On March 21, 1850 Vahíd was with his wife and four sons. He owned a palace in Yazd and because of his reputation and fame, he had a New Years party at this house. All the leaders, government officials and religious leaders were present. At this party Vahíd openly advanced the claim of his Master, the Báb. As his proofs of the truth of the Báb as the promised messenger of God were proven by the Holy Qur'án, and the accepted traditions no one dared to dispute the claim Vahíd made. The majority of those present readily accepted the truth of the Báb and became staunch believers. A few however fearful of losing their power over the people vowed in their heart to kill Vahíd. This mass conversion spread like wildfire throughout the area and for forty days Vahíd was busy from early morning until late at night teaching the thousands of people that came to his house.

Some of those that had been present at the New Years party banded themselves together with the sole purpose of killing Vahíd. They got together about one thousand men, mostly from the bad people of the city and this mob inspired by the disgruntled leaders were intent on attacking Vahíd in his house. A few men, whom no one even knew about suddenly appeared, and while Vahíd was still teaching the huge crowds from the balcony of his house, these few men attacked the mob and sent the them into hiding.

Four men were dispatched by Vahíd to go through the city of Yazd led by a man with a very strong and powerful voice to advise the crowd of his true intentions. This town crier caused the entire population of the city of Yazd to side with Vahíd. That very night Vahíd sent his wife and two of his sons to stay with her father and he had all of his friends leave him. Vahíd also slipped away and took the trail into the mountains. His sole purpose in leaving was to avoid further blood shed. Vahíd was mounted on the very horse that the King had given to him when he was sent to Shiraz to interview and investigate the teachings of the Báb.

All along the route Vahíd was accorded a welcome by the villages through which he passed and hundreds upon hundreds of people took up the cause of the Báb through the efforts of Vahíd. Upon arrival in a town, village or city the first thing Vahíd would do was go the Mosque and proclaim from the pulpit openly and fearlessly the teachings of His Holiness the Báb.

Vahíd also owned a house in Nayríz and as he approached this city on May 27, 1850, hundreds of people went out on the road to welcome him. The Governor advised the population of Nayriz that anyone helping Vahíd would lose their families, life and property. This advice of the Governor was ignored by all. Over fifteen hundred people in Nayríz alone accepted the teachings of the Báb at Vahíd's first meeting.

In the meantime the Governor sent word to Shiraz for the army which was duly sent to Nayriz. Vahíd and seventy two of his followers took refuge in a fort near Nayríz and were soon joined by many others. Now took place a repeat of Tabarsi. That is the failure of the army, and finally the dispatch of the Qur'án with a sworn statement of peace and safety to the defenders. As Quddús had done, Vahíd did also in respect for God's Holy Book the Qur'án. He left the fort and once again in violation of their sacred vows the entire company were put to death in a most horrible way. The death of Vahíd took place in Nayríz on June 29, 1850. Unlike the Tabarsi incident that lasted such a long time, the Nayríz incident lasted only for a month.

The central Government was now duly alarmed at the turn of events and although the imperial army had eventually won the day through deceit and trickery, they were convinced that the moving force Himself, the Báb, must be destroyed. Far from this fire going out, each encounter had given the Cause of the Báb additional fire in proclaiming His Divine Message and additional supporters.

The new prime minister under the new king, Náiri'd-Din Sháh sent an order to Chihriq, to the Governor to transfer the Báb once again to Tabriz. This Governor was a prince, and he had fallen under the spell of the Báb. The prime minister was very careful not to tell this Governor his plan to kill the Báb. The Governor was sure that this transfer was to release the prisoner.

The Báb, forty days before this order was received had sent His seals, pen case, rings and a scroll written in His own hand to Bahá'u'lláh. This scroll was written on a fine blue paper in the form of a five pointed star. It contained 361 derivatives of the word Bahá. This Governor took the Báb to Tabriz with the highest honor and respect and upon their arrival in Tabríz the Báb was housed in one of the homes of a friend. Three days after the Bábs arrival in Tabriz. This Governor received the order to suspend the Báb in the public square in the center of Tabríz and to execute Him at once, upon receipt of this royal decree. the Governor refused to do it. He stated that in no way would he even be a party to killing an innocent descendant of the Prophet of God. The messenger from Tihrán that brought this death warrant was then commanded to carry out the instructions from the prime minister.

Now according to the Islamic prophecy the first of the twin Manifestations of God that were to appear in the fullness of time, stated that He would be put to death by His fellow Muhammadans. Therefore the religious leaders in concert with the prime minister ordered that the Christian regiment under the command of Sam Khan do the killing, thus once and for all time they would lay to rest this false claim that the Báb was indeed this Promised One.

Sam Khan was ordered to remove the Báb from the house where He was staying and confine Him in the barracks in the center of the city. On the way from the house to the barracks two of the Báb's followers rushed into the crowd to meet Him. They were arrested and put into the barracks cell with the Báb and His secretary. Sam Khan then stationed guards at the door.

The secretary of the Báb was released the following day and he was an eye witness to what took place the night before. The Báb explained to the three men that the following day He was to be martyred such as happened to Jesus almost two thousand years ago. We must understand that the Báb was indeed the very Voice of God amongst men. Once we have acknowledged this Voice as the Voice of God, then what ever He says do, we must do. Whatever He says don't do we better not do.

The Báb ordered each of the three men in turn to arise and terminate His life right then, as He said that He would rather be killed by a friend than by an enemy. Just imagine ourselves in that position. Here is His Extreme Holiness the Báb (Gate of God), kindness to the extreme, loving, gentle, inspired and radiant. How would we react? Probably like the secretary and the next man. Our very souls would shrink from even the thinking of such an act. Anís the young man who had dreams and visions of the Báb long before they met, jumped to his feet and said " I am ready and I obey". The Báb took Anís into his arms and explained that he would be with Him throughout all the worlds of God and no separation would take place in this world or in eternity. Such is the reward for our obedience. All the participants in these events are gone and for the most part forgotten. In the same way we also one day will be gone and forgotten. If we are to be remembered at all it will be for what we have achieved in the service of God and the service of humanity.

Early the next morning the Chief of Police was ordered to take the Báb to all the leading high priests in the city for them to sign His death warrant. When the Chief arrived the Báb was engaged in talking to His secretary and giving him some final instructions. This Chief of Police rudely interrupted them and instructed the Báb's secretary to come with him. The Báb informed this Chief that no power on earth could stop Him from saying to the last word the things He had to say. The Chief of Police said nothing but took the secretary away anyway.

The Báb was conducted to each of the high priests homes in turn and each one of them refused to see the Báb or meet Him. They sent a servant to the door with the signed death warrant.

When all the needed warrants were signed and collected the Chief of Police delivered the Báb into the hand of Sam Khan for execution. In the meantime Sam Khan had become affected by his prisoner. He was suddenly filled with a great and overwhelming fear of the wrath of God. So he explained to the Báb that he was a Christian and did not want to shed His Holy blood. The Báb lovingly and gently told Sam Khan to go ahead and follow his orders and if in his heart he was sincere, God would deliver him from any blame.

So a big spike was driven into the wall of the barracks in the city center of Tabríz and Anís asked to be placed in front of the Báb that his body might afford a little protection. So it was arranged. Their wrists were tied together and they were thus suspended from the spike in the barracks wall. Sam Khan formed his regiment in three rows of two hundred and fifty rifles each. One row was prone, the second row was kneeling and the third row was standing.

Ten thousand people had assembled to

watch this execution. All the buildings, the barracks roof, and house tops were filled with people. In those days gun powder when fired gave off a very black smoke and when the explosion of the seven hundred and fifty guns were fired at the same time the cloud of smoke turned day into night. When the smoke finally cleared Anís was sitting on the ground and rubbing his wrists and the Báb was gone.

A frantic search was made and the Chief of Police found the Báb sitting in the same room finishing His conversation with His secretary. The Báb turned to this Chief and told him that He was finished and could now go ahead with his killing. The Chief of Police was severely shaken and resigned his job right then and left and reported what he had witnessed and participated in, far and wide. Sam Khan also remembering the words of His Holiness the Báb marched his men out of the square and vowed that he would die before he would make another attempt on such a precious life. The ropes that had tied them to the spike was shattered into pieces. The Báb and Anis were unharmed.

On the same wall and in the same manner the Báb and Anís were once more suspended and a Muslim colonel with his regiment of Muhammadans carried out the execution. The last words of the Báb before the shots were fired, He said. "Had you believed in me, O wayward generation every one of you would have followed the example of this youth, who stood in rank above most of you, and willingly sacrificed himself in My path. The day will come when you will have recognized Me; that day I shall have ceased to be with you." the shots of this second regiment of seven hundred and fifty guns once more boomed out over the city of Tabriz. At the same instant that the shots were fired, a whirl wind of exceptional velocity swept over the city blotting out the noonday sun and blinded the eyes of the people till night. The bodies of Anís and His Holiness the Báb were so riddled with bullets that they had merged into one flesh. Their faces had not been destroyed. It was the noon hour on July 9, 1850 and the Báb was thirty one years old. His earthly ministry lasted only seven short years. His spirit of love and truth and message is destined to last into the far distant reaches of time. At least five hundred thousand years.

Now another prophecy of Muhammad was that this Holy Manifestation of God that was to come when murdered by his Muslim brothers, His holy and immaculate body would be preserved from all beasts and insects and would become a holy shrine to which the whole world would flow and would become even a more sacred spot than the shrines of Mecca and Medina. This Muslim Clergy, that were well aware of these teachings of Muhammad, had the bodies of the Báb and Anís removed to the moat outside Tabríz where the wild dogs would eat them. The Russian Consulate had a sketch drawn of the Báb and Anís after their deaths. During the late watches of the second night the bodies were skirted away to a silk factory in Milan by one of the believers and sealed away in a wooden box. The guards claimed that while they slept the wild animals had dragged them away. The authorities for fear of the wrath of the high priests concealed the truth from them. Then Bahá'u'lláh had these remains transported to Tihrán where at His orders, they were moved from place to place, with the greatest secrecy. These remains arrived in the Holy Land on January 31, 1899. They were finally laid to rest on March 21, 1909 at the spot chosen by Bahá'u'lláh on Mount Carmel designated as "God's Holy Mountain". The beautiful golden dome rises from the heart of this mountain and already thousands of pilgrims from all over the world, pay their respects and offer their prayers at this Shrine of the Báb. It should also be remembered that in even their dust, Anís the voice of absolute obedience and the Báb receive this homage. When one visits this glorious shrine of the Báb they are also visiting the shrine of Anis.

The regiment that fired that fatal shot lost two hundred and fifty of their members when an earthquake occurred and they were buried alive under a wall. Also in that same year the remaining five hundred were shot in the public square of Tabriz before the eyes of the same people that had witnessed the death of the Báb. The prime minister that had initiated this cruel act fell from power and within two years met his death, murdered in the public bath by order of the King he was trying to serve. He was all alone and friendless. A great earthquake in 1852 devastated the entire city of Shiraz, over 7000 people died. All across Persia was famine, plagues and other dire afflictions that brought the entire country to its knees.

The martyrdom of His Holiness the Báb was the signal for a concerted effort by the clergy to root out and destroy any followers of His. Many innocent non-believers were killed in this holocaust. Anyone could accuse anyone else of being a Bábí and once accused, a tortuous death followed the accused. The accuser activated solely by the intention of stealing the others property.

In the historical work of the famous E.G. Browne it was stated, "Now in these years 1850 to 1851 throughout Persia fire fell on the house-holds of the Bábís, and each one of them, in whatever hamlet he might be, was, on the slightest suspicion arising, put to the sword. More than four thousand souls were slain, and a great multitude of women and children, left without protector or helper distracted and confounded, were trodden down and destroyed."

There lived in the city of Zanján a man named Hujjat. As a child Hujjat showed an exceptional scholarship. His keen intelligence excited the wonder of his family. His father sent him to Najaf to school and he attained the station of high priest. Upon his fathers death he returned to Zanján and as his father was also a very distinguished high priest, he was received with love and enthusiasm by the population of Zanján. For the next seventeen years he taught from his pulpit and insisted that his followers live in strict accordance with the divine text of the Qur'án. Those Hujjat taught had more exact knowledge of the Qur'án than the other leading religious figures in Zanján. Even more important they tried with heart and soul to live in accordance with those same teachings.

When Hujjat heard about the teachings of the Báb he had sent a messenger to get information and upon reading just one page of the writings of the Báb he became a firm and steadfast believer. The very jealous clergy of Zanján drew up a petition which they all signed and sent it to the King complaining about Hujjat. Because Hujjat was already famous the King decided to bring him to the capital along with his accusers where he would be able to judge the true situation. In this debate Hujjat won over the King and his hearers. The King rewarded Hujjat and publicly declared his complete innocence of the false accusations of the clergy of Zanján. Humiliated and defeated the hate of this clergy was made stronger and their efforts were redoubled. They continued their barrage of complaints to the prime minister and eventually, in order to keep peace, the King ordered Hujjat to the capital.

Many meetings were arranged for Hujjat in the capital and at each meeting he bested his opponents. He had the favor of the King and therefore his protection, however he was kept a prisoner and by the King's order was not allowed outside of Tihrán. At this time, like Vahíd, Hujjat spent as much time as possible with Bahá'u'lláh and received from Him inspiration and strength. When the call came for Tabarsi, Hujjat longed to go but because of the King's order, he could not go.

The King died and Hujjat knowing that the clergy and government officials now, without the protection of the king, would surely take his life, he left for Zanján.

Upon Hujjats arrival in Zanján a tremendous demonstration of love and affection and assurances of their undying support came from the people as they poured into his home. The Governor of Zanján was amazed at this great acclamation for Hujjat and jealousy was kindled in his heart. Then as often happens two small children got into a fight and the follower of Hujjat's child was arrested and taken into custody by the order of the Governor. Of course Hujjjat protested and wrote to the Governor asking that he release the child, stating that if blame was to be placed it should be placed on the father not on a small child. The Governor refused and ignored Hujjat. Hujjat then sent a messenger that induced the Governor to release the child. The priests then counseled the Governor to arrest Hujjat, stating that if he let himself be told what to do by Hujjat that there would be no end to his demands. So a group of men went to the quarters to make the arrest, when one of the Bábís raised the cry of "O thou Lord of the age!" and sprang forward and the whole group ran off in every direction.

Some members of this band found an unarmed Bábí on the street and broke his head with an ax. They then carried him to the Governor. One of those present stabbed him with a pen knife and the Governor struck this innocent and hapless victim in the mouth with his sword. The rabble then fell upon him and put him to death. His only crime was to be on the wrong street at the wrong time. This murder emboldened the mob to further violence and they determined to take the life of all the Bábís they could find.

The Governor sent a crier through the city warning the population that anyone who sided with Hujjat would endanger his life and property, expose his wife and children to shame and were advised to leave the area where Hujjat lived. The city of Zanján was divided into two camps. Husbands and wives separated, brothers also, and families were torn apart. Hujjat from the pulpit proclaimed in a strong and vibrant voice that this day the division was made between truth and falsehood. He further explained that the sole object of vengeance was himself, and that no one need place themselves into danger for his sake. The friends of Hujjat were advised that this was not to be a Holy War and they were only to defend themselves if and when they were attacked. Hujjat moved out of his house to a nearby fort along with his companions. This was May 16, 1850 while the Báb was still in Chihríq.

The Governor was able to raise an army of above three thousand men from around the local area. Also with Hujjat were about three thousand of his loyal followers. This was by far the largest group of Bábís, ever to come under attack. When the Governor informed the central Government of the situation two regiments were dispatched post haste for Zanján. Another officer that had been requested to go had flatly refused. He said that even at the cost of life he would never consider to make war on a band of students and men of learning. The feeling was spreading among the officers of the imperial army that the Báb was indeed the Promised One of the Qur'án.

The attack on the fort always brought out a response from the Bábís. They would rush out of the fort and raising that same cry of Tabarsí, "O Thou Lord of the age!" put the whole army and the recruits of the Governor to flight. After nine months only thirty crippled soldiers were left of the two regiments the officer had commanded at the beginning. The officer was humiliated and was degraded in rank. Although new regiments were being dispatched constantly they could not defeat the Bábís in the fort. The defenders had constructed twenty-eight barricades and at each barricade they had nine-teen Bábís on watch.

A young maiden named Zaynab who was in the fort with the other women and children cut off her long hair, dressed herself as a boy and shouting "O Thou Lord of the age!" attacked the enemy and sent them into flight. Hujjat, watching the attack recognized her. When questioned she explained that her heart ached with pity and sorrow when she beheld the suffering and hardships of her men companions and longed to help. For five months Zaynab rushed to the forefront of every battle. All the other Bábís were assigned a particular post that they were to defend but Zaynab was free to assist whenever and wherever the need existed. Day and night oblivious of sleep and hunger she would be found in the thick of battle. When she would find time to sleep, her shield was her blanket and her sword her pillow. Although the enemy finally discovered her identity her voice shouting out "O Thou Lord of the age!" still filled them with unimaginable terror as they abandoned their posts. It was in the fifth month of the struggle as this maiden was engaged in demolishing the barricades the army had put up when she was struck down in a hail of bullets and died instantly.

A great contrast was noted by many observers between the fort of the Bábís and the camp of the army. The Bábís used their time in prayers and supplications to God and chants and songs of God's love could be heard issuing from the fort by day and by night. In the camp of the army there was drinking (which was forbidden by Muhammad), gambling (also forbidden), shame and debauchery. The sounds from the army camp were noisy laughter, swearing, cursing and blasphemies.

As this conflict extended into weeks then into months, more and more troops were dispatched by the government to Zanjan. The final count was a total of seventeen regiments of Calvary and infantry and fourteen cannons. This long siege was slowly sapping the life of the Bábís, in just one encounter over three hundred Bábís were killed. In spite of the superiority of trained men and equipment they were unable to win the victory.

Taking an example from Tabarsí and Nayríz, the generals of the army dispatched a Qur'án with the same written promises. This time however Hujjat refused to be tricked and sent nine children the oldest was only ten with a delegation of the oldest in his camp all those were over eighty years old. A tall dignified man with white hair and a white beard led the delegation holding in his hand the Qur'án that had been signed and sent by the general of the army. This delegation upon arrival at the generals tent were all killed in a most vicious manner. One child escaped and made it back to the fort and reported all that had happened.

With the armies trickery and deceit uncovered they had no other alternative but to continue the assault and for one whole month the bombardment of the fort continued night and day. It was during this period that Hujjat was wounded in the arm. Shortly after Hujjat's wife and infant son were killed and nineteen days later Hujjat also passed away suddenly. When the army learned of the death of Hujjat they intensified their efforts and the struggle was over. It was recorded that over fifteen hundred Bábís were killed up to the death of Hujjat and over two hundred more were butchered after he was killed..

CHAPTER 11
Remnant of God

The following quote was made by the Báb about Bahá'u'lláh and was recorded by Bahá'u'lláh:
"O thou Remnant of God! I have sacrificed myself wholly for Thee; I have accepted curses for Thy sake; and have yearned for naught but martyrdom in the path of Thy love. Sufficient Witness unto me is God,"(Kitáb-i-Íqán, page 231)

"The Remnant of God will be best for you if ye are of those who believe." Qur'án 11:85

After the fall of Hujjat and the Bábís of Zanján and the killing throughout Persia of the innocent Bábís, it seemed that, as the prime minister had hoped, the cause of the Báb was being forever extinguished. Yet there was, **One Remanent of God**, the majestic and towering figure of Bahá'u'lláh.

The Prime Minister of the young King Náiri'd-Din Sháh, who had issued the death warrant of the Báb and was instrumental in the Tabarsi, Nayríz and Zanján upheavals, now directed his attention to Bahá'u'lláh. He called Bahá'u'lláh to the capital and there in polite but firm terms issued his orders banishing Bahá'u'lláh to Karbilá in Iraq. Bahá'u'lláh left Persia, as requested by the government, sometime early in August 1851. He continued the teaching work with wisdom and vigor during the nine months He was forced to stay in Iraq.

We are able to get a glimpse of the future greatness of Bahá'u'lláh through a recorded happening during this time. You will recall the incident earlier recorded when Siyyid Kazim had taken his student Hasan with him to visit the Báb at dawn. This Hasan later became a very devoted follower of the Báb. At the time of Tabarsí when the Báb had notified all the Bábís in Persia to go to the aid of the Black Standard and Mullá Husayn, Hasan who was then acting as a personal secretary to the Báb, in Chihríq prepared to go. The Báb stopped Hasan and explained that he had a much greater mission than Tabarsí. Hasan was directed by the Báb to Karbilá, Iraq with a sure promise that He was to meet Bahá'u'lláh, whom he would recognize. Hasan was instructed to extend the whole hearted love, respect and devotion from the Báb to Bahá'u'lláh. Hasan was further instructed to keep his mission an absolute secret. From Chihríq Hasan went to Karbilá as instructed, married and worked and waited. It was on October 5, 1851 that Hasan's eyes first gazed upon the figure of Bahá'u'lláh in Karbilá as promised by the Báb. Hasan gives a graphic description of this meeting: "What shall I recount regarding the face which I beheld! The beauty of that face, those exquisite features which no pen or brush dare describe, His penetrating glance, His kindly face, the majesty of His bearing, the sweetness of His smile, the luxuriance of His jet-black flowing locks, left an indelible impression upon my soul. Bahá'u'lláh took my hand and in a voice of power and beauty, said to me. 'Praise be to God that you have remained in Karbilá, and have beheld with you own eyes the face of the Promised One.' From that moment all my sorrows vanished. My soul was flooded with joy." This was the first recorded instance of the recognition of the true station of the King of Glory, Bahá'u'lláh.

It was the spring of 1852 and the prime minister that had initiated so much blood shed, the death of His Holiness the Báb, and the banishment of Bahá'u'lláh, was put to death by the orders of the King. His veins were opened in the public bath. The new Prime Minister at once dispatched a warm letter inviting Bahá'u'lláh back to Persia and ending His first banishment. Upon His return to Tihrán, Bahá'u'lláh spent a month as the house guest of the new Prime Minister. As it was now well into summer and with the excessive heat of the capital, Bahá'u'lláh headed for the mountains and a vacation home of the Prime Minister's.

Then three stupid and head strong men took it upon themselves to make an attempt on the life of the King. They loaded their pistols with bird shot and then waited on the road that they knew the King would take. This was August 15, 1852. These three assassins waited outside the palace in the district of Shimiran near Tihrán. They were dressed as gardeners near the garden of the Directory of the Treasury. This was the road the King would take going on his morning hunt. When the King emerged on his horse with his large staff and came opposite of the three they attacked. One on his right grabbed the bridle of the King's horse at the same time firing his pistol at the King. The two men on the left side of the King also got off their shots. All these shots that struck the King did not hurt him. The two men on the left now tried to pull the King off of His horse to dispatch him with their knives. At the firing of the shots and the lunge for the horse, the horse was frightened and wheeled away thus saving the King further injury. The body guard of the King now swung into action. The man on the right was cut down with a sword. The two on the left were quickly overpowered and tied up. These two declared that they were Bábís and were intent on avenging the death of the Báb.

    The Prime Minister's brother sent an urgent message to Bahá'u'lláh explaining the situation in the capital. Eighty-one Bábís had already been arrested and he urged Bahá'u'lláh to go into hiding. The situation was dangerous and explosive. In fact he explained that the mother of the King, the Queen mother, was openly accusing Bahá'u'lláh of being the one behind this attempt on her son's life. At this time, due to the mid-summer heat, Bahá'u'lláh was staying in the summer home of the Prime Minister.

Refusing this advice Bahá'u'lláh the next morning mounted His horse and started for the headquarters of the King's army. Bahá'u'lláh was met about ten kilometers from the army headquarters by His brother-in-law who was a secretary to the Russian Consul. The Russian Consul Prince Dolgorukov was a close friend of Bahá'u'lláh. This Consul sent Bahá'u'lláh directly to the home of the Prime Minister with a message that Bahá'u'lláh was now under the protection of the Russian Government and He should be treated accordingly. The Prime Minister gave the Russian Consul his word that Bahá'u'lláh would be protected and safe. The Prime Minister was also being denounced by the Queen mother as one of the would be murderers of her son. The government was amazed that Bahá'u'lláh had come to them and sent the police to arrest Him. The Prime Minister disregarding his promises to the Russian Consul, turned Bahá'u'lláh over to the police.

Bahá'u'lláh was chained in heavy chains and forced to walk in the heat of a mid-summer sun all the way to Tihrán. The sun blazing down, one of the guards snatched off Bahá'u'lláh's hat, He was hurried along bare footed and bare headed and the crowds lined the road leading into the Capital. They jeered, shouted and pelted Him with rocks and garbage. One old woman with a rock in her hand ran to catch up so that she might throw her rock. The procession was moving to fast for her. Bahá'u'lláh stopped in the road and told the guards to let her throw her stone, as in her eyes this was a great thing to do in the path of God. This whole scene was a repeat of that time when Jesus Christ was being taken to His crucifixion.

The Black Pit, also called in Persia the Síyáh-Chál, located near the palace in Tihrán was to be the place of confinement. It was used in former times as a water reservoir for a public bath. It was then changed into the worst prison in the land. Bahá'u'lláh was taken down a pitch black hall, then down three steep flights of stairs. The only exit being the trap door that opened up above their heads. He who was used to sunlight and countryside and had grown up free and of noble birth, was almost overcome with the foul smell and the putrid air of the place, added to this was the utter pitch black darkness. He was then weighted down with a steel collar and chain that weighed fifty-one kilograms and the chain was secured to the floor. There were around one hundred and fifty prisoners in this pit, about forty of them were Bábís that had been arrested. All the prisoners were chained together. The throat that had been accustomed to silk and satin was scarred for life by the horrendous chain. There were no facilities for the human waste and the lice, insects and rats added to the prisoner's misery. Bahá'u'lláh had neither food nor drink for the first three days and nights.

One of Bahá'u'lláh's servants carried the news to His family. He came running to the wife crying that the Master had been arrested, had walked with torn clothes and burning and bleeding feet and His body bruised from the stones and sticks of the people along the road into Tihrán. He was now a prisoner in the Black Pit. Bahá'u'lláh was thus imprisoned for a period of four months. Every day one of the Bábís would have his name called out and he would be unchained and be put to death often in the most fiendish manner. All these men had to do to secure their freedom, was to declare in a public statement that the Báb was not the Promised One from God. This they did not do and preferred to die rather than deny the truth of their Lord. This blood bath was not confined to Tihrán alone but spread out across the land. Every corner of Persia saw the Bábís and those that were accused of being Bábís were murdered. Some times whole families including the children were butchered. So another famous tradition of Muhammad, about the promised teacher from God, "His saints shall be abased in His time, and their heads shall be exchanged as presents, they shall be slain and burned and the earth shall be dyed with their blood; these are My saints indeed."

The fickle and untrustworthy Prime

Minister not only encouraged the killings throughout the land, but took this opportunity to steal some of Bahá'u'lláh's property and to transfer some of His assets to his own name. The Russian Consul was enraged that the Prime Minister had violated his trust in protecting Bahá'u'lláh. The Russian Prince used his influence, and along with many other honest and upright men they defended Bahá'u'lláh. The tribunal proved beyond any doubt that He was totally innocent of that foul deed of attempted murder of the King. The King and his mother wanted Bahá'u'lláh dead but the fear of Russia and these leading government officials stopped him from going that far.

In this Black Pit, with the putrid and foul air, the black darkness, the icy chill, the insects and vermin, weighted down with unbearably heavy chains, feet in stocks, insufficient food and His companions being murdered each day, the light of God in the form of a Maiden announced the station and mission of God to Bahá'u'lláh.

Bahá'u'lláh was created by God for this divine mission. Like the dove coming from heaven and landing on the shoulder of Jesus Christ when He was in the river Jordan with John the Baptist; with the angel Gabriel that came to Muhammad; the seven visions of Zoroaster; so it was with Bahá'u'lláh. The following account is taken from the words of Bahá'u'lláh:

"While engulfed in tribulations I heard a most wondrous, a most sweet voice, calling above My head. Turning My face, I beheld a Maiden the embodiment of the remembrance of the name of My Lord suspended in the air before Me. So rejoiced was she in her very soul that her countenance shone with the ornament of the good pleasure of God, and her cheeks glowed with the brightness of the All Merciful. Betwixt earth and heaven she was raising a call which captivated the hearts and minds of men. She was imparting to both My inward and outer being, tidings which rejoiced My soul, and the souls of God's honored servants. Pointing with her finger unto My head, she addressed all who are in heaven and all who are on earth, saying: "By God! This is the Best Beloved of the worlds, and yet ye comprehend not. This is the Beauty of God amongst you, and the power of His sovereignty within you, could ye but understand. This is the Mystery of God and His Treasure, the Cause of God and His glory unto all who are in the kingdoms of

Revelation and of creation, if ye be of them that perceive." (God Passes By page 101-102)

Although the King, the Queen mother, the Prime Minister and some of the leading men of the court were intent on putting Bahá'u'lláh to death, they did not consider the power of God that was protecting Him. Bahá'u'lláh received divine assurances about His safety directly:

> "These exalted words were heard on every side: 'Verily, We shall render Thee victorious by Thyself and by Thy Pen. Grieve Thou not for that which hath befallen Thee, neither be Thou afraid, for Thou art in safety.' (Epistle to the Son of the Wolf, page 21)

When the murders were stopped there were only three Bábís left alive in that prison. One of them, Bahá'u'lláh. Although very ill and suffering, His blessed body scarred for life from the grueling weight of the chains He was soon to be released. Due mostly to the stern and courageous action of the Russian Consul, Prince Dolgorukov. He asked for permission to address the court that was issuing these death sentences. Permission was granted and he boldly proclaimed to that court:

"Hearken to me! I have words of importance to say to you. Have you not taken enough cruel revenge? Have you not already murdered a large enough number of harmless people, because of this accusation, the absurd falsity of which you are aware? How is it possible that you can even pretend to think that this august prisoner planned that silly attempt to shoot the Shah? You know very well that this charge is not only untrue, but palpably ridiculous."

"There must be an end to all this. I have determined to extend the protection of Russia to this innocent nobleman; therefore beware! For if one hair of his head be hurt from this moment, rivers of blood will flow in your city as punishment. You will do well to heed my warning. My country is behind me in this matter."

Russia had defeated Persia in the war of 1804-1814 and again in the war of 1826-1828 and the King and the Persian government knew that the Russians were looking for any excuse to extend their borders even further into Persia. Although Prince Dolgorukov may have been bluffing the Persian government dared not take a chance on this. Bahá'u'lláh was ordered released. The order from the King was for Bahá'u'lláh's immediate release and the order of the King was His banishment for life from Persia. The sight that greeted the dignitary that was sent to release Bahá'u'lláh caused him to openly weep. He cursed the Prime Minister and the government for their cruel treatment of Bahá'u'lláh. Here was this man of a noble family, whose life had been dedicated to helping others, chained to the floor in the stinking hole, His body bent under the heavy chain, the vermin and insects everywhere, His face still shinning with glory of His new revelation, but also showing the gaunt and sickness of the four months in prison. This dignitary offered Bahá'u'lláh new clothes to wear, but Bahá'u'lláh refused. He presented Himself to the Prime Minister in the rags of the prisoner. Bahá'u'lláh very sharply condemned the Prime Minister for his lack of justice and his corruption. Bahá'u'lláh, even in His sad condition was able to persuade the Prime Minister to cease and stop killing any more innocent people. The Prime Minister that very day in the middle of December issued a national order to stop the slaughter.

By this royal order of banishment, all of Bahá'u'lláh's vast wealth and property was taken by the government. What had not been robbed before by the thieves and looters was in this way taken from Him. This decree also gave Bahá'u'lláh and His family only one month to leave Persia forever. Not only did He turn away from the country of His birth but also away from His wealth and worldly treasures. A true example for all mankind to follow into the far distant future. For us to put our complete trust and confidence in God and not in this temporary world and its fast disappearing materials.

From the vast estates and palatial houses, Him and His family now lived in two tiny rooms.

Bahá'u'lláh (The Glory of God), illuminated by the very Spirit of God in the Black Pit of Tihrán was now on the road to the full-filling of prophecy. Not by choice but by an Imperial decree forcing Him onto this road to Baghdad in Iraq.

CHAPTER 12
Táhirih

The one lone woman who had declared her belief in His Holiness the Báb based on a dream she had, was not spared in this holocaust that engulfed Persia after the attempt on the life of the King. Táhirih was born into one of the leading religious families of Qazvin. Her father was one of the highest ranking high priests of that area. She was born in 1817 and much like Bahá'u'lláh she lived a sheltered and protected life in the most luxurious setting. It was not custom in Persia for girls to be educated, but Táhirih showed such a high degree of intelligence that her father taught her to read and write. Later on he even hired a special tutor for her. As she grew her thirst for knowledge also increased.

At the tender age of thirteen she was married to her cousin and her father-in-law was also a high priest of great position. Táhirih's husband was being educated to take his fathers place. We have very little information about this period of her life. We do know that she had three children, two boys and a girl. We also know that she read the books in her husbands and father-in-law's library. When ever she had the opportunity to listen to the discussions on the Qur'án and traditions of Muhammad she would sit behind the curtain and listen. In Persia women were considered almost like animals. They were to be used to satisfy the needs of the men and contribute to their happiness. This they must do by not being seen or heard from. With her excellent and inquisitive mind this was most difficult for Táhirih to do.

Táhirih found some books written by Shaykh Ahmad in her cousin's library. She borrowed these books and with her keen intelligence and inspired mind she saw the truth in this holy man's teachings. Her father objected most strongly to her reading these books. Táhirih began a secret correspondence with Siyyid Kazim. With her deep and penetrating vision and her vast knowledge of all the traditions and the Holy Qur'án, her new teacher, Siyyid Kazim gave her the name "Solace of the Eyes". She determined to meet Siyyid Kazim in person and left her native city, home and family in the fall of 1843. She arrived in Karbilá on January 10, 1844 just ten days after the death of her beloved teacher. Siyyid Kazim.

Táhirih was a very beautiful young woman of twenty six upon her arrival in Karbilá. She then joined the group of students of Siyyid Kazim and spent her days in prayer, meditation and discussions preparing herself to seek out and find the Promised One of God. It was in Karbilá that she had her dream of the Báb and sent the message with her brother-in-law (sister's husband) to Him and was enrolled by the Báb as one of the nineteen letters of the living. The first nineteen to accept Him as the promised Teacher from God. As you will remember from an earlier chapter Táhirih woke up from that dream and wrote down the verse that the Báb was writing. Later after her declaration as one of His followers she found that exact same verse in the first writings she received from the Báb.

For three months Táhirih translated the teachings of the Báb and saw to there widest possible distribution. Every day her home in Karbilá was besieged by the crowds that came to hear this marvelous woman and to learn from her. She then moved to Baghdad and stayed in the house of the Mayor of the city and continued with the utmost strength and vigor to teach the Cause of the Báb. Here she remained for about three months. She stayed in Baghdad until the message was received from the Báb addressed to all of His followers to join Quddús and Mullá Husayn in Khurasan. At this same time she got a message from her father ordering her to return to Qazvin. As Qazvin was on the road to Khurasan she agreed and all along the route she won the hearts of vast numbers of people to the cause of the Báb.

In Qazvin Táhirih went directly to her father's house. Her husband sent word ordering her to his house. She refused and in her reply stated, "Three years have elapsed since our separation. Neither in this world nor in the next can I ever be associated with you. I have cast you out of my life for ever." This reply caused the husband and father-in-law to declare that she was a heretic and should be put to death. Her father tried to effect a reunion but failed. Táhirih was well aware of her ex-husbands and father-in-laws base and mean character and their trampling on the divine principles of the Holy Qur'án in the name of their so called high positions.

A follower of Shaykh Ahmad and Siyyid Kazim named 'Abdu'lláh from Shiraz was passing through the city of Qazvin and as he drew near the city center he saw a crowd had gathered. When he could get close enough to see what was going on, he saw a man stripped of his clothes with the cloth of the turban wound around his neck. This man was being dragged and beaten by the mob. Others were jeering and cursing him. 'Abdu'lláh asked what was this mans crime to receive such harsh punishment. He was informed that this man in public had been teaching the writings of Shaykh Ahmad and Siyyid Kazim. The high priest (Táhirih's father-in-law) had declared him a heretic and had ordered this severe punishment.

'Abdu'lláh was amazed at this explanation and he went directly to the high priest and asked him about it. Táhirih's father-in-law confirmed the report. 'Abdu'lláh in his heart was enraged however, he said nothing. He went back to the market and purchased a dagger and a spear-head of fine steel. He vowed in his heart to pierce the lips of the high priest that said such things about these two proven holy men, that was Shaykh Ahmad and Siyyid Kazim.

Then 'Abdu'lláh waited until dawn when the high priest came to the Mosque. An old woman came in first and put down a prayer rug and soon the high prist entered alone and went to the rug and started his dawn prayer. 'Abdu'lláh came up behind him and drove his spear-head into the back of the high priests neck. He then turned him onto his back and drove his dagger up to the hilt in the high priest's mouth and stabbed him in several other parts of his body. 'Abdu'lláh then climbed up to the roof and watched. Soon the crowd gathered and everyone was accusing everyone else of this foul deed. The Governor had a large number of people arrested and thrown into prison.

'Abdu'lláh went directly to the Governor and said that if he was to turn over the real culprit would the Governor let the other innocent people that were arrested go free. The Governor agreed and 'Abdu'lláh confessed. The Governor did not believe him even when the old woman agreed that it was him. They took 'Abdu'lláh to the bedside of the dying high priest and he confirmed that it was indeed 'Abdu'lláh. So passed away the father-in-law of Táhirih. Although 'Abdu'lláh was not a Bábí and had no connection whatsoever with the Bábís. They were the focus of attention. In the meantime, with the aid of a friend, 'Abdu'lláh escaped from prison when he learned that the Governor refused to let the innocent people go free.

Táhirih's husband and his relatives were insisting that this was her work and she was the instigator of the murder. The Governor had the people that were arrested moved to Tihrán. The owner of the house where these people were confined contacted Bahá'u'lláh and told Him that these innocent people were not being fed and were in deplorable condition. Bahá'u'lláh at once gave him money to assist these people. The owner of the house then went to the authorities and said that Bahá'u'lláh was one of the guilty parties and was supplying money and food to the victims. Bahá'u'lláh was confined for a short time because of this slander. His first confinement. Most of the people that were confined in Tihrán were later murdered by the high priest's relatives.

Táhirih was also confined to her fathers house under strict guard. The mobs were now intent on putting her to death. As soon as Táhirih was informed of this intention she wrote a letter to her ex-husband. In this letter she declared, "If my Cause be the Cause of Truth, If the Lord whom I worship be none other than the one true God, He will within the next nine days have set me free of your tyranny. Should He fail to set me free, you are free to do with me as you want." This challenge went unanswered by her ex-husband, but traveled on the wind across Persia. Bahá'u'lláh then arranged to have a woman disguised as a beggar to go to the place of her confinement. This woman was to give a message to Táhirih. She was instructed by Bahá'u'lláh to wait for Táhirih who would soon come out of the side entrance. These two women were then to go to the city gate of Qazvin accompanied by one of Bahá'u'lláh's trusted servants. Out side this gate Bahá'u'lláh had three horses waiting. He ordered His servant to follow His instruction very carefully and assured him that God would aid and protect them. They were then to ride non-stop as fast as the horses could go directly to Tihrán. They must arrive at the gate of the capital as soon as the gate was opened in the morning. They were ordered directly to Bahá'u'lláh's home. This distance is about 130 KM from Qazvin to Tihrán. The disguised beggar woman was not noticed and as they slipped away from Táhirih's father's house they were not seen by the guards. They were not stopped at the city gate of Qazvin nor at the gate of Tihrán, although both gates were heavily guarded. The next morning a frantic search was made for Táhirih, house to house, in Qazvin but she was no where to be found. The people that were aware of Táhirih's challenge were convinced that a miracle had taken place and the angels of God had taken her away.

Táhirih was now under the sheltering protection of Bahá'u'lláh and as Vahíd and Hujjat had stayed with Him so did she. She was able to get that love and inspiration from Him and she was well aware of the future station of Bahá'u'lláh and openly mentioned Him in her poems and writings. In fact Táhirih and Vahíd were house guests of Bahá'u'lláh at the same time. As the Bábís from all over the country and as far away as Iraq and India were responding to the orders of the Báb to go to Khurasan and join Quddús and Mullá Husayn, Bahá'u'lláh made arrangements for Táhirih to start for there and He was also making plans to go.

In Khurasan in the city of Mashhad where Quddús and Mullá Husayn were holding their classes such a tremendous influx of people could not help but alarm the authorities. The chief constable had Mullá Husayn's special attendant arrested. They cut a hole in his nose and putting a string through the hole paraded this attendant through the streets of Mashhad. Against the advise of Mullá Husayn a number of Bábís banded together and for the first time the cry of "O Thou Lord of the Age" was raised by this band in Mashhad. The people that were parading this hapless attendant through the streets were killed. Mullá Husayn was requested to come to the army camp where a special tent had been put up to receive him. He was received by these officers with a dignity and respect that was outstanding. The same day that Mullá Husayn left for the army camp, Quddús left for Mazindaran to meet Bahá'u'lláh when he learned that He was coming.

Bahá'u'lláh had smuggled Táhirih out of

Tihrán undetected and He soon followed. It was the start of the summer of 1848 and Bahá'u'lláh had rented three gardens in a place called Badasht. He assigned one garden to Táhirih, another for Quddús and the third for Himself. This historic conference is historically called the "Conference of Badasht", it was here that all the laws and teachings of the Báb were put into effect and a complete break was made from the past laws and traditions of Islam. There were eighty one participants and under the direction and skill of Bahá'u'lláh this break was made. The conference lasted 22 days. Táhirih, who was in the eyes of the Bábís, the very emblem of chastity and the most saintly of women suddenly appeared among these believers without her veil. The new teaching of His Holiness the Báb of the equality of women was in this way shown to the believers by this courageous woman, Táhirih. Bahá'u'lláh also gave each person a new name and later when some of the Bábís complained to the Báb about this action of Táhirih in taking off the veil. The Báb said, "What can I do when the Tongue of Power and Grandeur has named her Táhirih." Táhirih means the pure one. After this conference when the Báb wrote to the participants He addressed them according to the new names that Bahá'u'lláh had given them.

Quddús explained that it would not be in accord with wisdom for them to go on to Khurasan as planned because of the volatile situation. When these participants in the conference of Bada<u>sh</u>t left Quddús, were captured and made prisoner. Bahá'u'lláh went to His summer home in the province of Nùr. The other Bábís returned to their homes. It was reported that Táhirih, intent on lending her help to Mullá Husayn, was in the city of Barfurù<u>sh</u> in September of 1848. She was in hiding in that vicinity about a year. She was betrayed and her host killed and she was taken to Tihrán in January 1850. It was at this time while a prisoner in the capital in the home of the mayor that she also was allowed to visit Bahá'u'lláh again.

Táhirih continued to teach the cause of the Báb while in the Mayor's house and won over completely the wife and children of the Mayor. This wife was instrumental in introducing Táhirih to the influential women in the capital. A steady stream of visitors came to see her and learn. In early September 1852 after the attempt on the life of the King, Táhirih had three interrogations by some leading priests in Tihrán and was again convicted as a heretic and condemned to death. The wife of the Mayor left her written account of this event:

"One night, while Táhirih was staying in my home, I was summoned to her presence and found her fully dressed in a gown of snow-white silk. Her room was filled with the smell of the sweetest perfume. I expressed my surprise at so unusual a sight. 'I am preparing to meet my Beloved,' she said, 'and I wish to free you from the cares and problems of my imprisonment.' I was startled at first, and wept at the thought of being separated from her. "Weep not,' she said. 'I wish to share with you my last wishes, for this night I will die. I would request you to allow your son to accompany me to the scene of my death and to ensure that the guards and executioner into whose hands I shall be delivered will not compel me to divest myself of this attire. It is also my wish that my body be thrown into a pit, and that the pit be filled with earth and stones. Three days after my death a woman will come and visit you, to whom you will give this package which I am trusting to you. My last request is that you permit no one to enter my room. From now until when I am called to leave your house let no one disturb my prayers.'

The great love I had for her in my heart, alone enabled me to do as she had asked. I locked the door to her room. That day and evening I often stood silently at her door. I was enchanted by the sweetness and the melody of her voice as she chanted her prayers. Four hours after sunset, I heard a knocking at the door. I went to my son and told him of the wishes of Táhirih. My son opened the door and told me that the officers of the Minister of War was at the door demanding me to turn over Táhirih. I opened her door and found her veiled and ready to go. As soon as she saw me she came to me and kissed me. She placed in my hand the key to her chest and advised me that the things in the chest were mine.

Three hours later my son returned, his face drenched with tears, cursing the Minister and his officers. 'Mother,' through his tears he explained, 'I can scarcely attempt to describe what my eyes have beheld. We straightway went to the Ilkhani garden outside the city gate. There I found to my horror, the Minister of War and his officers absorbed in acts of debauchery and shame, flushed with wine and roaring with laughter. Táhirih got off of her horse, calling me to her she asked me to be her intermediary with the Minister. She did not want to see them in their condition. 'They apparently wish to strangle me,' she said. 'I set aside, long ago, a silken kerchief which I hoped would be used for this purpose.'

When I went to the Minister I found him in a state of wretched intoxication. 'Interrupt not the gaiety of our festival!' He shouted at me. 'Let that miserable wretch be strangled and her body be thrown into a pit!' "

There was a well in that garden that was not finished so Táhirih was strangled and her body lowered into that well and the well filled with stones and earth. Her last words to an uncaring world was. "You can kill me but you will never stop the emancipation of women."

So ends the opening tale of the most magnificent story ever to be told by man. As foretold over one thousand years ago the lovers of

God in the last days would be killed, their heads exchanged as gifts. Between twenty and thirty thousand people willingly sacrificed their precious lives in Persia in the name of His Holiness the Báb and the King of Glory Bahá'u'lláh. Like shooting stars, these heroes of God blazed a trail of glory across the Persian sky. Vanishing as they had lived in a most glorious tribute to love, peace, unity and brotherhood.

All alone stood the towering figure of Bahá'u'lláh. Truly the "Remnant of God".

Chapter 13
King of Glory

January 12, 1853 saw Bahá'u'lláh and His family leaving Tihrán forever. His baby was too young and frail for such a journey in the middle of a severe winter so he was left behind with relatives to care for him. As most of their property had been either stolen or confiscated by the government they were not properly prepared for such a trip. Also Bahá'u'lláh did not have sufficient time to recover from His ordeal of four months in the Black Pit of Tihrán. This banishment of Bahá'u'lláh reminds us of the banishment of Abraham to the promised land, the banishment of Moses in Egypt, and the flight of Muhammad from Mecca to Medina. A representative of the Persian Government and a representative of the Russian Government were commissioned to go with Bahá'u'lláh and His family to Iraq.

The road they had to take was over rugged mountains, high plateaus and snow clogged mountain passes. The winter of 1853 was a very severe winter. Bahá'u'lláh wrote:

> "Thy behest summoned this servant to depart out of Persia, accompanied by a number of frail-bodied men and children of tender age, at a time when the cold is so intense that one cannot even speak, and ice and snow

so abundant that it is impossible to move." (God Passes By page 108-109)

So the Light of God, the Redeemer of Mankind, the Lord of the Age, and the King of Glory, Bahá'u'lláh, He who had given from His great heart, love, justice, mercy and helped and cared for the poor and under-privileged of Persia left their country. Him and His little band arrived in Baghdad, Iraq on April 8, 1853.

A written description of the greatness and power of Bahá'u'lláh as recorded during this early time in Baghdad by a man that later was to become His secretary follows: "How shall I ever describe that voice and the verses it intoned, and His gait, as He strode before me! Methinks, with every step He took and every word He uttered thousands of oceans of light surged before my face, and thousands of worlds of incomparable splendor were unveiled to my eyes, and thousands of suns blazed their light upon me! In the moonlight that streamed upon Him, He thus continued to walk and chant." (God Passes By page 115-116)

It was one year that Bahá'u'lláh taught and strove with heart and soul to rejuvenate the Báb's followers in Baghdad. Then one morning on April 10, 1854 Bahá'u'lláh was gone. No one had any idea of where He had gone not even His family, His friends nor His enemies. Like all of the Manifestations of God in the past He had gone into the wilderness. Like the forty days that Christ went into the wilderness of Judaea, Buddha in the wilderness in India and Muhammad in the deserts of Arabia so Bahá'u'lláh went into the uninhabited wilds of the mountain of Sulaymáníyyih. Separated from all contact with anyone, in complete solitude He prayed, meditated and communed with His Spirit. For two years Bahá'u'lláh had little or no contact at all with mortal man. He stated that often the days passed without any food and He lived in the caves three days away from the nearest inhabitants. Although at times Bahá'u'lláh wept tears of agonizing sorrow for wayward and Godless humanity, at other times He stated that His soul was surrounded by blissful joy. The birds and beasts of the field were His only companions.

One day as Bahá'u'lláh was near a Kurdish town He found a small child sitting by the side of the trail crying. When He asked the child what was the matter the child said that he had lost his copy the teacher had given him and he would be punished. Bahá'u'lláh told the child not to cry as He would set a new copy for him. Bahá'u'lláh sat down on the side of the trail and set the copy. When the child took it to school the teacher was amazed at the most beautiful writing he had ever seen. This copy then was shared with the religious leaders of that area. They immediately dispatched a delegation to seek out Bahá'u'lláh. The asked Him many questions and were profoundly impressed with His knowledge and wisdom. These religious leaders then requested Bahá'u'lláh to move into the seminary in the city. The fame of Bahá'u'lláh on the wings of the spirit soon was known far and wide and a large number of divines, leaders and students came to him for truth and guidance.

Although Bahá'u'lláh was not using His real name, His fame soon reached Baghdad and several people were sent to beg Him to return. Bahá'u'lláh consented and His peace and quite solitude came to an end. As the longest period of any previous messenger of God was forty days we can well imagine the effect of Bahá'u'lláh's retirement for such an extended time will be on the future of mankind. He returned to Baghdad on March 19, 1856 almost two years after he had departed.

Bahá'u'lláh upon His return to Baghdad reinvigorated the Bábis and slowly won over the respect and admiration of most of the notables of the city. Some few for reasons of self interest and personal gain arose to do him harm. This group led by the Persian Consul to Baghdad put out a hit contract on the life of Bahá'u'lláh. This hit man waited until Bahá'u'lláh was left alone in the public bath. He then entered the bath and when he came close to Bahá'u'lláh he later explained, "When I found myself in the presence of Bahá'u'lláh, I was so struck by awe and remorse that I turned on my heel and fled." This same hit man in order to earn his fee made another attempt on the life of Bahá'u'lláh. This time he waited at a vantage point on the route that Bahá'u'lláh took when He visited a coffee house. He waited pistol in hand. Bahá'u'lláh appeared in the distance only accompanied by one friend. He became so perplexed that he dropped his pistol and was unable to move. When Bahá'u'lláh came level with him, He told His companion to pick up the man's pistol, give it back to him and to help him back to his home, as he seemed to have lost his way.

A group of about a hundred ruffians were then recruited and they disguised themselves as mourners going to a funeral and they were to mount an attack on Bahá'u'lláh at His home. When the mourners approached the house of Bahá'u'lláh, He had the door opened and invited them in. He served them sherbet and tea and when they left they had become friends instead of enemies. As in His youth, Bahá'u'lláh was also known in Baghdad as the father of the poor. No one who sought help was refused and the poor and helpless Bahá'u'lláh would seek them out on His own and take care of them.

Due to the unrelenting efforts of the Persian Consul, the government of Persia began to press the Iraqi government to remove Bahá'u'lláh from Baghdad, as they said it was too near the frontier of Persia. Eventually this pressure bore fruit and Bahá'u'lláh was sent an invitation to come to the capital in Istanbul as a guest of the government.

Bahá'u'lláh accepted and the money that had been sent to cover the cost of his travel He gave it all to the poor of Baghdad that same day. On a beautiful spring day, April 22, 1863, Bahá'u'lláh left Baghdad for a garden on the further bank of the Tigris river. The road and river bank was crowded with people that came to say farewell to one they had grown to love over the ten years since His arrival in their city. There were representative from the highest to the poorest that were seen weeping at His departure.

The garden where Bahá'u'lláh had his tent pitched was filled with rose bushes and they were all in bloom with the most beautiful roses. Every day during the twelve days that Bahá'u'lláh stayed in that garden, the gardeners would pick the roses and they would be piled up so high that one could not see over them. Bahá'u'lláh would give these beautiful and most fragrant roses to the throngs of people that came to express their sorrow at His departure and say good-by.

It was during this period that Bahá'u'lláh openly proclaimed to His close followers that He was the one foretold and promised by God. The One promised by all the teachers and prophets of God, from Adam up to and including the Báb. Bahá'u'lláh, The Prince of Peace, The Voice of God and the return of the Spirit of God into the world.

The party of travelers that went with Bahá'u'lláh numbered seventy two. This caravan was shown the greatest respect and consideration everywhere they stopped. Bahá'u'lláh was mounted on a red roan stallion of the finest quality and He seemed to be a King of Kings with His small band on the road to Constantinople. Bahá'u'lláh when in Tihrán was in the capital of the Shí'ah branch of Islam. On August 16, 1863, Bahá'u'lláh arrived in the capital of the Sunní Branch of Islam the two most powerful centers of the religion of Muhammad. Bahá'u'lláh was received as a guest of the government with dignity and respect. He had traveled a long distance over mountains, rivers, and deserts and had even journeyed over the black sea to reach Constantinople. This was the great city of Constantine the Great.

After Bahá'u'lláh declared His divine mission in Baghdad he changed. There was a steady stream of visitors from government officials to the poor and needy that He saw. He spent the rest of His time in revelation. That is, He was busy from day to day in writing. He dispatched tablets and answered questions. Although a guest of the government He refused to follow the accepted practice of visiting the government officials and seeking favors and paying bribes.

They were in Constantinople for only four months when Bahá'u'lláh was ordered by the Sultan to go to Adrianople. There was no reason given nor explanation as to why. This order was not an invitation to go but an order issued by the Sultan. So the banishments of Bahá'u'lláh continued. He was banished from Tihrán the capital of Persia by the King and now He was being banished from the capital of Iraq by the Sultan. Once again He was taken prisoner. Bahá'u'lláh was also being banished from the continent of Asia to the continent of Europe. This was the first time in the entire history of religion when a major messenger of God would set foot in Europe.

When this order was received by Bahá'u'lláh, He wrote a tablet to the Sultan. This was the first King to be addressed directly by Bahá'u'lláh. The Government official who delivered this message to the Prime Minister of the Sultan wrote about this message as follows:

"I don't know what that letter said, for no sooner had the Prime Minister read it than he turned the color of a corpse, and remarked. 'It is as if the King of Kings were issuing His behest to His humblest vassal King and regulating his conduct.' So grievous was his condition that I backed out of his presence."

Bahá'u'lláh had sent most of His followers and the Bahá'ís that had come to visit him in Constantinople away. So on December 12, 1863 Bahá'u'lláh arrived in the city of Adrianople. The city He said that no one enters except those that have rebelled against the authority of the King. He called it the "Remote Prison".

The writings of Bahá'u'lláh increased and it was in Adrianople that He wrote His famous letters to the Kings, rulers, religious leaders, and peoples of the world. Once again people from Persia were making the long and difficult trip to visit Bahá'u'lláh. A steady stream of visitors were once more pouring into Adrianople. The enemies of Bahá'u'lláh continued to feed false reports to the government. One of these enemies Bahá'u'lláh's half brother even succeeded in poisoning Him, the results left Bahá'u'lláh with a shaking hand until the end of His life.

Early one morning soldiers suddenly appeared and surrounded the house of Bahá'u'lláh and would not let anyone enter or leave the house. The Bahá'ís were all called by the government and questioned. Those that admitted being Bahá'ís were forced to sell all their possessions. The ones that had gone into business were treated the same. The result was that everything was auctioned off by the government and only a small percentage of the value was received by the Bahá'ís. The people of Adrianople were amazed and many went to the police and asked them what these people had done. They had found them all to be the most truthful, trustworthy and religious people in the city. The foreign consuls one and all came to Bahá'u'lláh and offered to assist Him. Bahá'u'lláh thanked them and advised them that His Cause was the Cause of God and He was entirely in the Hand of God. The guards tried to stop these Consuls from entering Bahá'u'lláh's house but were unable to do so. An eye witness to this event stated: "The high Turkish officials were scandalized and infuriated by the preferential treatment of those foreign representatives. The easy access they had to the person of the eldest Son of Bahá'u'lláh riled them, particularly as the government officials when they tried to enter were put off on some pretext and not allowed in. The head official threatened the troops with a severe punishment if they failed to stop these foreign consuls from entering the next day. The following day these foreign consuls came as usual and the guards could not stop them. When these consuls were told of the government threats one of them said, 'They might ask the British consul to lead the way next time to receive the beating promised by the government official'. As to this officer that had made the threats, his superiors were displeased and reprimanded him, for they realized their impotence to prevent the visits of the foreign representatives, who continued to come and go whenever they wished."

A few months less than five years Bahá'u'lláh had lived in Adrianople, His Remote Prison and His land of Mystery. It was in this city that Bahá'u'lláh had proclaimed His divine mission to the world, from Europe went the summons of God, not from Asia. It was on August 12, 1868, in company with a contingent of soldiers, Bahá'u'lláh left as a prisoner for Akka in the Holy Land. He arrived on the Austrian-Lloyd ship August 31, 1886.

So once again the Holy Land was blessed by a Manifestation of God within it. The land promised by God to Abraham. The city that King David had called "The Strong City" and David had further said, "and the King of glory shall come in. Who is the King of glory? The Lord of hosts, He is the King of glory". Hosea had named the "Door of Hope". Ezekiel said, "And, behold, the Glory of the God of Israel came from the way of the east: and His voice was like a noise of many waters: and the earth shone with His Glory." Muhammad had promised, "Blessed the man that has visited Akka, and blessed he that has visited the visitor of Akka."

The son of Bahá'u'lláh made an interesting statement, he said,

> "When Bahá'u'lláh came to this prison in the Holy Land, the wise men realized that the glad tidings which God gave through the tongue of the prophets two or three thousand years before, were again manifested, and that God was faithful to His promise; for to some of the Prophets He had revealed and given the good news that 'The Lord of Hosts should be manifested in the Holy Land.' All these promises were fulfilled; and it is difficult to understand how Bahá'u'lláh could have been obliged to leave Persia, and to pitch His tent

in this Holy Land, but for the persecution of His enemies, His banishment and exile." (Some Answered Questions page 31-32)

The Prophet Micah had foreseen, ".... and from the fortified cities, and from the fortress even to the river, and from sea to sea, and from mountain to mountain, He shall come." So Bahá'u'lláh (The Glory of God) did come. From the Black Pit of Tihrán to the Tigris and Euphrates river, from the Black sea to the Mediterranean sea and from the Mountains of Sulaymáníyyih to Mount Carmel. Even from Continent of Asia to the continent of Europe He came, not of His own free will but as a prisoner of two corrupt Kings. The promise of God was in every detail fulfilled by the coming of Bahá'u'lláh to Israel.

The royal order that was read out in the city of Akka upon the arrival of the prisoners stated that they were to be imprisoned for life and were accused of leading other people astray and they were forbidden by this decree from associating with others and even with each other. A copy of this royal decree is still available. This decree was still in effect and was used even after Bahá'u'lláh's life was finished against His eldest son 'Abdu'l-Bahá until 1912 when due to a revolution and the overthrow of the government the decree became null and void.

In the beginning these rules were most

strictly observed but little by little they were relaxed and in the end the government officials and population were won over to love and respect for Bahá'u'lláh and the Bahá'ís. After nine years confined to the prison, Bahá'u'lláh left the prison of Akka and no one opposed Him. Later a large mansion was first rented and then purchased for Bahá'u'lláh at a place called Baji and it was here on the May 29, 1892 Bahá'u'lláh left this earthly plane for His heavenly kingdom.

The teachings of Bahá'u'lláh have now spread clear across this planet earth even into the remote jungles and islands of the world as I write this, Kings, Prime Ministers and leaders of the world are consulting with the members of the supreme body ordained by Bahá'u'lláh for solutions to the problems facing a fast evolving world.

*****THE END*****

www.ingramcontent.com/pod-product-compliance
Lightning Source LLC
Chambersburg PA
CBHW020903090426
42736CB00008B/479